PENGUIN CLASSICS

THE SECRET HISTORY

PROCOPIUS was born at Caesarea, the great city built b
on the coast of Palestine. We do not know the date: it was ꜥ
AD 500 or a little before. In 527 he was appointed private
and legal adviser to Belisarius, whom he accompanied o
three campaigns, in Persia, Africa and Italy. When Belisaꜥ
capturing Ravenna, was recalled to Byzantium, Procoꜥ
with him, and it is probable that when in the next year bₑ
was again sent to the eastern front his secretary once more accompanied him. But twelve months later, in 542, he was certainly
back in the capital, where he witnessed the terrible plague which
visited that city. We do not know whether he was with the general
during the years of his second campaign in and around Italy, or
what he did with his time, apart from literary work, during the
remaining years of his life. The date of his death is not known,
but he may have outlived Justinian. From Procopius' pen three
works have come down to us, commonly known as the *History
of the Wars*, the *Buildings* and *The Secret History*.

G. A. WILLIAMSON was born in 1895 and was a Classical Exhi-
bitioner at Worcester College, Oxford, graduating with a First
Class Honours degree. He was Senior Classics Master at Norwich
School from 1922 to 1960. He also translated *Josephus: The
Jewish War* (1959) and *Eusebius: The History of the Church*
(1965) for the Penguin Classics. He died in 1982.

PETER SARRIS was born in 1971 and educated at St Albans School
and Balliol College, Oxford, graduating with a 'Double First'. He
was elected a Fellow of All Souls College, Oxford in 1993, and is
now University Lecturer in Medieval History and a Fellow of
Trinity College, Cambridge.

PROCOPIUS

The Secret History

Translated by G. A. WILLIAMSON *and* PETER SARRIS
with an Introduction and Notes by PETER SARRIS

PENGUIN BOOKS

PENGUIN CLASSICS

Published by the Penguin Group
Penguin Books Ltd, 80 Strand, London WC2R 0RL, England
Penguin Group (USA) Inc., 375 Hudson Street, New York, New York 10014, USA
Penguin Group (Canada), 90 Eglinton Avenue East, Suite 700, Toronto, Ontario, Canada M4P 2Y3
(a division of Pearson Penguin Canada Inc.)
Penguin Ireland, 25 St Stephen's Green, Dublin 2, Ireland
(a division of Penguin Books Ltd)
Penguin Group (Australia), 250 Camberwell Road, Camberwell, Victoria 3124, Australia
(a division of Pearson Australia Group Pty Ltd)
Penguin Books India Pvt Ltd, 11 Community Centre, Panchsheel Park, New Delhi – 110 017, India
Penguin Group (NZ), 67 Apollo Drive, Rosedale, North Shore 0632, New Zealand
(a division of Pearson New Zealand Ltd)
Penguin Books (South Africa) (Pty) Ltd, 24 Sturdee Avenue, Rosebank, Johannesburg 2196, South Africa

Penguin Books Ltd, Registered Offices: 80 Strand, London WC2R 0RL, England

www.penguin.com

First published in Penguin Classics 1966
This revised translation first published 2007

013

Translation copyright © G. A. Williamson, 1966
Introduction and Notes, and revisions to the translation, copyright © Peter Sarris, 2007
All rights reserved

The moral right of the editor and translator has been asserted

Set in 10.25/12.25 pt PostScript Adobe Sabon
Typeset by Rowland Phototypesetting Ltd, Bury St Edmunds, Suffolk
Printed in Great Britain by Clays Ltd, St Ives plc

ISBN: 978-0-140-45528-1

www.greenpenguin.co.uk

Contents

Introduction

Of the literary forms and traditions that the modern world owes to the ancient Greeks, perhaps none has done quite so much to shape contemporary intellectual attitudes as the writing of history. To seek to understand the causes and origins of the world around us, to explain the evolution of that world in rational terms and to appreciate and empathize with the complexity and frailty of the human condition, irrespective of the race, creed, or class of the individuals concerned, are key characteristics of the modern Western mind that stem directly from the Greek historiographical perspective. History, in short, was one of the great glories of Greek culture, and of all the historians to have written in Greek, Procopius of Caesarea stands out as one of the greatest.[1]

Procopius is our primary literary source for the reign of the sixth-century Byzantine (or Eastern Roman) Emperor Justinian I (527–65), whose period of rule stands out from the pages of Roman and Byzantine history for its energy, ambition and forcefulness. From his imperial capital at Constantinople (Byzantium), Justinian sought to restore Roman rule to the provinces of Africa, Italy and Spain, which had been lost in the fifth century to military usurpers and barbarian invaders. At the same time, he faced a belligerent foe to the east in the form of the ancient empire of Sasanian Persia. At home, Justinian set about the codification and reordering of the inherited tradition of Roman law and the restructuring of provincial government.

1. This Introduction owes much to Professor Cyril Mango, whose lectures on Byzantine historiography I had the privilege to attend whilst an undergraduate at Oxford in the early 1990s.

Religious affairs also demanded his attention, as the imperial Church increasingly found itself wracked by bitter disputes over the nature of the relationship between the Human and the Divine in the person of Christ.

In spite of the vast detail of historical evidence concerning Justinian's reign to be found in the legal compilations which he ordered to be produced, the large number of documentary sources that survive from his period of rule (albeit mostly preserved in the sands of Egypt) and the rich vein of archeological evidence, Justinian is nevertheless known to us chiefly through the writings of Procopius, who, by contrast, emerges as a relatively shadowy figure. Of Palestinian origin, he was born in the city of Caesarea, presumably around the turn of the sixth century. He clearly received an excellent education in the Greek classics, although where we do not know. The quality of his education would suggest that he was probably born into a relatively wealthy family. In addition to Greek he is likely to have had a fair amount of Latin and presumably some Aramaic or Syriac (the indigenous language of the region). He is usually described in the sources as a jurist or legal advocate – a *rhetor*. The first post we know that Procopius held was as *assessor* (military legal secretary) to the general Belisarius, whom he accompanied on campaign against the Persians between 527 and 531. In the year 533–4, Procopius again travelled alongside Belisarius as the latter led the Byzantine reconquest of Vandal North Africa. Procopius remained in North Africa under the general Solomon from 534 to 536, in which year he once more joined Belisarius, this time on his Italian campaign. Procopius remained in Italy until at least 540, by which point he would have spent a good thirteen or fourteen years on the military front line, witnessing direct active service. In the year 542–3 he found himself in Constantinople, where he witnessed at first hand the advent of bubonic plague – the first onslaught of this disease in the history of the Mediterranean. Thereafter his movements are unknown. In the early 560s we do hear of a Procopius who served as Urban Prefect of Constantinople, but whether he is to be identified with Procopius the historian is far from clear.

Procopius of Caesarea was thus a widely travelled man who was present at many of the events which he was to go on to describe in his histories. It was this wealth of first-hand experience, feeding into a rare and striking breadth of vision, that permitted him to write autoptic, 'classicizing' history after the manner of Thucydides – a point which he emphasizes at the very start of Book 1 of his *History of the Wars*, where he declares that he 'had assurance that he was especially competent to write the history of these events, if, for no other reason, because it fell to him, when appointed adviser to the General Belisarius, to be present at practically all the events he described'.[2] Procopius' account of the battle of Dara between Belisarius and the Persians in 530 is the first eye-witness account of a battle written by a Roman author since Ammianus Marcellinus in the fourth century.

Procopius' writings can be divided into three. First (and the basis of his great reputation) we have his multi-volume *History of the Wars*, detailing Justinian's wars against the Persians, Vandals and Ostrogoths respectively. Second we have his account of Justinian's building projects and commissions (known as the *Buildings*). Lastly, we have his *Anecdota*, or 'Secret History' (more properly 'Unpublished Writings'). As we shall see, the dates of composition of these various works are important.

We know that the first to be written was the *History of the Wars*, which Procopius began by 545 at the latest. This work was published in seven books, arranged geographically, to which he later added an eighth. He wrote two volumes on the Persian Wars, taking his coverage up to the year 548–9; there followed two volumes on the Vandalic Wars and the consolidation of the Byzantine position in North Africa, taking readers up to 548; three volumes on the Gothic Wars then take one up to *circa* 551. These various volumes were meant to constitute a single history. When Procopius came to write his eighth volume, the geographical basis on which he had been working had to be abandoned. Instead he provided an integrated narrative

2.   *Wars* 1.1.3.

detailing operations on all fronts between 548 and 553. He explained this change of approach in the *proemium* to Book 8:

> The account which I have written up to this point has been composed, as far as possible, on the principle of separating the material into parts which relate severally to the countries in which the different wars took place, and these parts have already been published and have appeared in every corner of the Roman Empire. But from this point onwards I shall no longer follow this principle of arrangement. For after my writings had appeared before the public, I was no longer able to add to each the events which happened afterwards.[3]

These words imply that during Procopius' lifetime his works enjoyed a wide readership and a distinguished reputation. Certainly, the *History of the Wars* received the early medieval equivalent of rave reviews. Agathias, Procopius' continuator in the task of charting the military fortunes of the Byzantine state from 553 to 558, cites him with great approval and evident respect, even if disagreeing with him on occasional points of detail.[4] In 590 the diplomatic historian Menander the Guardsman declared of Procopius, 'I am not able, nor do I wish, to hold up my candle before such a beam of eloquence.'[5] The late sixth-century ecclesiastical historian Evagrius was heavily reliant on Procopius and cites him as the main authority on the reigns of both Justin I (518–27) and Justinian, praising him for writing 'most assiduously and elegantly and eloquently.'[6] In the eighth century the chronicler Theophanes frequently drew on Procopius' accounts of the Persian and Vandalic wars, although he would not appear to have been aware of the existence of the

---

3. *Wars* 8.1.1–2.
4. See Averil Cameron, *Agathias* (Oxford: Oxford University Press, 1970); J. D. Frendo (trans.), *Agathias: The Histories*, Corpus Fontium Historiae Byzantinae (Berlin: De Gruyter, 1975).
5. R. C. Blockley, *The History of Menander the Guardsman* (Liverpool: Francis Cairns, 1985), Fragment 14.
6. M. Whitby, *The Ecclesiastical History of Evagrius Scholasticus* (Liverpool: Liverpool University Press, 2000), 4.12.

volumes on the Italian campaigns.[7] In the ninth century Photius
– the great humanist and Patriarch of Constantinople –
recorded that he had read all eight volumes of the *History of
the Wars*;[8] he praised what he described as 'the eternal glory
of Procopius'. In the tenth century Procopius' works were
excerpted for inclusion in the Middle Byzantine encyclopedia
known as the *Suda* lexicon. All three of his works survive in an
abundant manuscript tradition – indicating long-lasting popularity and acclaim.[9]

Beyond the intrinsic interest of the narratives, the reasons for
the popularity of Procopius, or at least his *History of the Wars*,
are reasonably plain to see. Although there is necessarily a
certain amount of stylistic repetition, his Greek is relatively
clear and accessible. Certainly, if one reads his *History* end to
end it is difficult not to come away with enormous respect for
the author's mastery of prose. In spite of his personal involve-
ment in so many of the events he describes, and his inevitable
partisanship, he nevertheless has the ability to detach himself
from the matter of History, to empathize not only with his
colleagues but also with his enemies, and to convey the exhausted, and somewhat embittered, sense of triumph felt by the
Byzantine army after the final conquest of Italy in the early
550s whilst also giving the reader a sense of the bravery, nobility
and dignity of the defeated Ostrogoths. We weep for them just
as Homer induces us to weep for the fallen Trojans. Indeed, in
many ways it is the Ostrogoths who emerge as the real heroes
of the work.

If all we had of Procopius' writings was his *History of the
Wars*, his standing as a historian of the first order would be
unchallengeable, and he would take his place with ease alongside Herodotus, Thucydides and Polybius. It is perhaps to the
detriment of his posthumous reputation, but to the enormous

7. C. Mango and R. Scott, *The Chronicle of Theophanes* (Oxford: Oxford
    University Press, 1997).
8. See the excerpt in N. Wilson, *Photius: The Bibliotheca: A Selection*
    (London: Duckworth, 1994), fol. 63.
9. *Wars* survives in twelve MSS, *Secret History* in five MSS and *Buildings*
    in three MSS.

benefit of subsequent generations of scholars and historians, that his two other known works have survived, and it is these works which, on face value, turn him into a rather more complicated character. The *History of the Wars* is normally understood as a work glorifying Justinian's military achievements, a work the initial hero of which is Belisarius. It is a secular history, written in a classicizing style (that is to say, in a classicizing prose style modelled on the likes of Thucydides and adopting an essentially antiquarian vocabulary) which shows no interest in religious affairs and fails to take an explicitly Christian line on anything.

The *Buildings*, by contrast, is a rather strange work and, in the form in which we have it, clearly incomplete. In its most complete early chapters it combines a sort of sustained panegyric celebrating the ecclesiastical and military structures built under Justinian which, in places, includes detailed virtuoso *ekphraseis*, or descriptive accounts of individual monuments and their visual impact on the viewer – most notably the structure of the cathedral church of Hagia Sophia. The preface to the work further glorifies Justinian's military triumphs and his legal reforms. As Procopius declares, '. . . in our own age has been born the Emperor Justinian, who, taking over the state when it was harassed by disorder, has not only made it greater in extent, but also much more illustrious.'[10] And then we have Procopius' vitriolic *Secret History*, in which he lambasts Justinian as a demon-king, an inveterate destroyer of established institutions and a compulsive liar, married to a former whore with voracious sexual appetites, in particular a predilection for group sex.

There is no doubt that all three of these works are by the same author. There are textual references within them to one another, they are written in an identical form of accentuated Greek prose, and they share other profound stylistic similarities, drawing upon the same grid of classical textual references, allusions and vocabularies. The question that has often perturbed historians is: Which of the three 'voices' represents

10. *Buildings* 1.1.6.

Procopius' true opinion? How are the three works to be reconciled?

One approach has been to suggest that Procopius' opinion of Justinian and his regime altered and evolved over time.[11] In the early years of the Emperor's reign, one might imagine Procopius – a lawyer by training and a military man by vocation – to have been excited by the rhetoric of imperial renewal, of the restoration of Roman law to its pristine glory and of the re-establishment of Roman rule over rightly Roman territories. This initial enthusiasm may have given way to growing disillusionment as the reality of Justinian's centralizing and autocratic tendencies became clear, and as the Emperor's parsimony had an ever more pronounced impact on the army's effectiveness. This disillusionment, it has been suggested, culminated in the *Secret History*. On this model, the *Buildings* is to be explained either as evidence that Procopius then changed his mind again with regard to the regime, perhaps as his own career advanced, or is to be accounted for as an imperial commission in which the author was obliged to hide his true feelings.

The main problem with this developmental approach to the Procopian oeuvre is that most of his works appear to have been written within a relatively narrow time span. *Wars* 1–7, as we have seen, were composed between *circa* 545 and 550 and *Wars* 8 between 548 and 553. On a number of occasions the *Secret History* locates itself as having been composed in the thirty-second year of Justinian's reign.[12] Since Procopius presents Justinian's reign as having effectively begun with the accession of his uncle Justin to the throne in 518, this would give a date of composition for the *Secret History* of *circa* 550 (i.e. coeval with *Wars* 1–7). Certainly, the work describes no single event that can be firmly located in the 550s.[13] Most commentators would place the date of composition of the *Buildings* as some time before 558, as it makes no mention of the collapse of the

11. As in J. B. Bury, *History of the Later Roman Empire*, vol. I (London: Macmillan, 1889), chap. 24.
12. E.g. *Secret History* 23.1
13. See G. Greatrex, 'The Dates of Procopius' Works', *Byzantine and Modern Greek Studies* 18 (1994), pp. 101–14.

dome of Hagia Sophia which took place in that year as a result of structural weaknesses in its eastern arch. In other words, the developmental interpretation leaves too little time for Procopius' opinions of the Justinianic regime to have evolved.

An alternative, and highly influential, analysis has viewed Procopius' texts primarily through the prism of the genres in which he wrote.[14] As a 'classicizing' author, the argument runs, Procopius was obliged to express himself through the structural media of specific inherited classical genres: the military history (*Wars*), the panegyric (*Buildings*) and the *psogos*, or invective (*Secret History*). The problem from Procopius' perspective was that no single one of these was sufficient to express the complexity of life in sixth-century Byzantium, or to fully convey his own opinions. So, for example, because traditional military narratives were meant to eschew discussion of such extraneous matters as religion, Procopius (on this model) supposed Christian piety and assumed religious interests could not find proper expression in his *History of the Wars*. Each of the genres in which he wrote enabled him to express some aspects of his world-view whilst, it is argued, rendering him mute on others. As a result, no one 'voice' can be said to be more authentic than any other.

To this a number of relatively straightforward responses can be made. First of all, in terms of genre, Procopius *chose* to write his *History of the Wars* in an inherited form which excluded religious considerations. This genre perhaps represented something of a literary safe haven for those conservative elements within Byzantine society who were unhappy or ill at ease with aspects of the Christianization of the inherited classical culture. It is striking that no Greek author writing in the 'High Style' – the Atticizing Greek of the Roman Second Sophistic – took an explicitly Christian line on anything until the seventh century. That is to say, the expressly Christian point of view only really emerged as triumphant and dominant once the traditional, classical urban centres of the Empire which had produced and

14. As thought-provokingly pioneered by Averil Cameron in *Procopius and the Sixth Century* (London; Duckworth, 1985).

preserved the conservative elite and which served as the *locus* for the replication of their culture had been destroyed amid the carnage brought first by the Persian invaders of the early seventh century and by the violent expansion of Islam thereafter. Had Procopius wanted to write a history that would have given him freedom to express his supposedly profound Christian sentiments, he could quite easily have chosen to write in the other historical genre that was to prove so popular in the Byzantine world: the Christian world chronicle. Such chronicles sought to place contemporary history in the context of the workings of Divine Providence, tracing events back to Creation and anticipating the Day of Judgement. Exactly such a choice was made by Procopius' contemporary and, it would appear, social analogue, John 'the *rhetor*' or John Malalas (Syriac for *rhetor*): an imperial, legal, military official from the great metropolis of Antioch in Syria.[15]

So if Procopius did not discuss religious affairs in much detail in his *History of the Wars*, it was perhaps because he did not want to. Certainly, divine providence is mentioned once in the *Secret History* (28.13). On a number of occasions he suggests that he is minded to write an *Ecclesiastical History* (e.g. 1.14). He refers not only in general terms to 'the divine' but also, specifically, to 'God' (e.g. 3.30). He may well have been a Christian, of a sort, but if so he was not a terribly doctrinaire one. In both the *Secret History* and the *History of the Wars*, whenever religious issues arise we see Procopius adopting an essentially enlightened, sceptical approach, dismissing fanaticism in all its forms. At one point, mentioning an embassy sent to the Pope by Justinian concerned with the interminable Christological dispute that was the main source of rancour within the sixth-century Church, Procopius interjects that he will not discuss the matter in any detail, as to him it is 'a sort of insane folly to investigate the nature of God'. 'I will keep silent on this matter,' he continues, 'that those matters held in respect should not appear discredited.'[16] Likewise, he is decidedly

15. See E. Jeffreys, M. Jeffreys and R. Scott (eds), *Studies in John Malalas* (Sydney: Australian Association for Byzantine Studies, 1990).
16. *Wars* 5.3.6–9.

cool regarding the persecution of Samaritans by Justinian in his
native Caesarea. It is, to him, an unnecessary act of cruelty and
violence. But Procopius praises those Samaritans who, rather
than face death, made a nominal conversion to Christianity.
He admires their pragmatism: '. . . the more willing converted,'
he states, 'thinking it foolish to endure any sort of distress for
the sake of a senseless creed' (11.25). A similar tone is adopted
in the *Secret History* with respect to Justinian's persecution of
astrologers. Procopius does not defend the astrologers, but he
regards their persecution as excessive. From both the *Secret
History* and the *History of the Wars*, therefore, the same picture
emerges. Procopius was not terribly interested in religion, did
not believe in persecuting people for their religion, but felt that
if faced with persecution, one should be pragmatic and toe the
line: after all, it was *only* religion. Given the consistency of his
views as expressed, we should perhaps be willing to accept
them as genuine.

Perhaps the most striking feature of Procopius' writings is
how *little* constrained by genre he actually was. It is true that
the *History of the Wars* is a 'classicizing' military history after
the manner of Thucydides. Procopius is engaged in much more
than a mere slavish copying of classical models, however. He
borrows and adopts different templates, approaches and epi-
sodes from different classical authors and recasts them to suit
his own purposes. Thus his account of the advent of the bubonic
plague in Constantinople in 542 may draw for its vocabulary
on Thucydides' account of the Athenian pestilence of 430 BC
(probably smallpox), but he uses that vocabulary to construct
an account of what is clearly a very different disease. The
Buildings is generically a very unusual work that defies easy
classification. As already seen, the *Buildings* combines elements
of the panegyric and the architectural *ekphrasis* before breaking
down into little more than lists of buildings (on the basis of
which one might imagine that it was still being 'worked up'
when Procopius died).

Of the three works, the *Secret History* is the most unusual,
however. Certainly, we know that ancient and medieval authors
did indeed write invectives, or *psogoi*. Most of those that sur-

vive are in the form of pithy epigrams or scurrilous verse lampoons. Passages of prose invective occasionally make their way into Middle Byzantine chronicles, such as that of the continuator of Theophanes, or *Theophanes Continuatus*. But none of these bear comparison to the *Secret History* either in length or in form. At over 150 pages of Greek text (and some 45,000 words or so in English translation), it is a remarkably sustained assault. It would appear to have been composed on an essentially tripartite structure (and it is in this form that the translation is presented here). The work opens with a *proemium* that bears every sign of having been reconstructed by an editorial hand on the basis of the preface to Book 8 of the *History of the Wars (Secret History* 1.1.). We then encounter Part I proper (here entitled 'The Tyranny of Women'). Comprising the first five chapters of the work, the main protagonists in this part are Belisarius and his wife Antonina, and the Emperor Justinian and his consort Theodora. The main theme is the emasculation of the Roman state and the deleterious consequences for mankind when women take charge of affairs. Much of the vocabulary here, and many of the literary allusions, are derived from the world of Greek comedy, in particular the plays of Aristophanes. Yet these comic elements are framed by narrative structures that bear close resemblance to those encountered in the Greek novel, most expressly the motif of star-crossed lovers separated by circumstance (in this instance Antonina and her toy-boy Theodosius).[17]

The second, and most notorious, part (chapters 6–18) is the most straightforwardly invective. These chapters are carefully calibrated pieces of character assassination aimed at the Emperor and his wife. They are essentially constructed on the basis of direct inversions of the accepted literary model of the imperial encomium or panegyric as codified in the third century AD by the rhetorician Menander.[18] Thus whereas the

---

17. See K. Adshead, 'The Secret History of Procopius and Its Genesis', *Byzantion* 63 (1993), pp. 5–28.
18. See L. Brubacker, 'Gender and Society', in M. Maas (ed.), *The Cambridge Companion to the Age of Justinian* (Cambridge: Cambridge University Press, 2005), pp.427–47.

model of the imperial panegyric demanded that encomiastic accounts begin with a paean to the nobility of the Emperor's family and an account of any miraculous events associated with his birth, Procopius tells us of Justinian that his parents were peasants of barbarian descent and that his mother was rumoured to have been impregnated by a demon. Theodora receives very similar treatment, with the added dimension that she is presented as an inversion of the ideal Roman matron. Thus whereas the Roman lady should be chaste in youth and faithful in marriage, Theodora is described as the cheapest of tarts who began life as a child-prostitute and to the end of her days was a slave to her passions (9.6–8). The ideal Roman matron should be retiring and demure; Theodora even dared to laugh and joke in public (9.14). The ideal Roman lady should be a devoted mother; Theodora aborted every foetus she could and eventually murdered the one son whose abortion had been botched (9.19, 10.3, 17.16–23). As a recent commentator has put it, '. . . in Theodora, Procopius created the perfect anti-woman.'[19] Instead of describing the good fortune and prosperity that the rule of noble sovereigns brings to the commonwealth, this part closes with an account of universal mayhem and natural catastrophe (18).

The final, more sober and historically perhaps most informative part of the work begins with a critique of Justinian's legal and fiscal reforms. Here it is often (although not always) possible to connect the specific accusations levelled by Procopius with extant imperial legislation. It is in this section that Procopius the lawyer is at his most visible. The critique then proceeds to analyze the impact of these policies on different sections within society – civil servants; great landowners; soldiers; merchants; lawyers, doctors and teachers; beggars and the poor – and then, once again, their impact on the effective workings of government.

The *Secret History* is thus a startlingly original composition, the author of which shows very little sign of having been constrained by anything, let alone genre. We quite simply know of

19. Brubacker, 'Gender', p. 424.

no other text like it. Be it in relation to the *History of the Wars*, the *Buildings* or, above all, the *Secret History*, Procopius comes across as an extraordinarily creative author who was able to take the inherited literary forms of antiquity and rearrange, recombine and reappropriate them in ways that look novel. We should note that the compiler of the *Suda* lexicon was unable to come up with a single all-embracing category under which to describe the *Secret History*: he had to label it as both invective and comedy.[20] Rather than the mute prisoner of classicism he is sometimes presented as, Procopius had a creative and far from reverent approach to the inherited classical genres. He was post-classical in the way that some authors today are post-Modern.

So which of Procopius' writings does represent his 'true voice'? He tells us in the preface to the *Secret History* that in his other accounts (meaning the *History of the Wars*) he had been obliged to conceal the full narrative of events, as it would have been too dangerous to reveal all. It is thus in the *Secret History* that he purports to relate what he really thinks. There are good reasons, prima facie, to take Procopius at his word, not least of which is the fact that the differences between these two works are more often apparent than they are real. The main one is that whereas criticism of Justinian and his policies in the *Secret History* is invariably explicit and direct and expressed in the authorial voice, in the *History of the Wars* the self-same accusations tend to be put into the mouths of others, such as foreign ambassadors or visitors to court, or are expressed implicitly, by way of literary allusion. Another ruse employed in the *History of the Wars* is to take charges levelled at Justinian in the *Secret History* and project them onto the Persian Shah Chosroes (Khusro). Justinian and Chosroes become, in effect, interchangeable as models of oriental despotism. Underpinning both works are the contours of a fundamentally hostile attitude towards the Emperor and his regime. The real problem is not so much how we reconcile the *Secret History* with the *History of the Wars*, but rather how we reconcile this

20. A. Adler (ed.), *Suidae Lexicon*, vol. IV (Stuttgart: Teubner, 1935), p. 211.

hostility with the posture adopted by Procopius in his *Buildings*.

Yet even in relation to the *Buildings* an underlying hostility to Justinian and his works may be discernible. It was noted earlier that most commentators date the composition of the *Buildings* to 558 on the grounds that in that year the dome of the Hagia Sophia collapsed, and no explicit mention of this is made in Procopius' account. Yet the closer one looks at his account of the building of Hagia Sophia, in particular that of the problematic eastern arch, the more suspect it becomes.[21] Procopius provides a lengthy and detailed description of how, during the arch's construction, the piers supporting it began to crack. In despair the Emperor's chief architects took news of this to him. 'And straightaway,' Procopius records, 'the Emperor, impelled I know not by what, but I suppose by God (for he is not himself a master-architect) commanded them to carry the curve of the arch to its final completion. "For when it rests upon itself," he said, "it will no longer need the props beneath it."'[22] When further problems developed with the masonry between other arches and the dome, Justinian again intervened. 'These instructions,' Procopius notes, 'were carried out, and thereafter the structure stood secure. And the Emperor in this way enjoys a kind of testimonial from the work.'[23] Given what Procopius had written of Justinian in his *Secret History*, imagine with what relish he would have penned these words in the full knowledge that both the divinely inspired eastern arch and the testimonial dome were eventually to collapse.

21. *Buildings* 1.1. 65–73.
22. *Buildings* 1.1.71.
23. *Buildings* 1.1.78.

Note on the Text

I present here a substantially revised version of G. A. Williamson's very fine translation of 1964 complete with new notes and suggestions for further reading. The structure of the translation has been much overhauled. I have removed the chapter headings which Williamson introduced and have instead divided the work on the tripartite model set out above, using numbers in square brackets to indicate chapter breaks in the Greek. Monetary sums have been returned to their sixth-century originals; the word barbarian used by Procopius but eschewed by Williamson has been reintroduced; and some of the textual emendations which Williamson rejected I have accepted. In general I have not sought to 'modernize' the translation – Procopius, after all, wrote in an antiquated linguistic register which had little in common with the demotic of his day. In some places I have drawn the translation rather closer to the original. This is particularly so with the more sexually explicit passages in parts I and II. In Part III, above all, both Williamson and the translator of the Loeb text, H. B. Dewing, frequently misunderstood important aspects of legal, fiscal or social terminology and as a result misconstrued crucial passages. Here too I have attempted to be much more precise. In the notes I have attempted to flag the more interesting of the literary allusions and the more significant cross-references to Procopius' other writings. Where specific laws are alluded to, I have sought to provide precise details (some but not all of which have been noted by A. Kaldellis in his recent study of Procopius; see Further Reading). As a result, I hope the revised text will be not only of interest to the general reader but also of use to the student.

PROEMIUM

[1] In recording everything that the Roman people has experienced in successive wars up to the time of writing, I have followed this plan – of arranging all the events described as far as possible in accordance with the actual times and places. But from now on I shall no longer keep to that method: from here on in I shall set down every single thing that has happened in every part of the Roman Empire.[1] The reason for this is that it was out of the question to tell the story in the way that it should have been recorded as long as those responsible for what happened were still alive. For it was impossible either to avoid detection by swarms of spies or if caught to escape death in its most agonizing form. Indeed, even in the company of my nearest relations I felt far from safe. Moreover, in the case of many of the events which in my previous writings I did venture to relate, I dared not reveal the causes for what happened. So in this part of my work I feel it is my duty to reveal both the events hitherto passed over in silence and the causes for the events already described.

But as I embark on a new undertaking of a difficult and extraordinarily baffling character, concerned as it is with Justinian and Theodora and the lives they lived, my teeth chatter and I find myself recoiling as far as possible from the task; for I envisage the probability that what I am now about to write will appear incredible and unconvincing to future generations. And again, when in the long course of time the story seems to

---

1. This opening passage would appear to be the work of a later editorial hand and modelled on the *proemium* to Book 8 of Procopius' *History of the Wars*.

belong to a rather distant past, I am afraid that I shall be
regarded as a mere teller of legends or listed among the tragic
poets. One thing, however, gives me confidence to shoulder
my heavy task without flinching: my account has no lack of
witnesses to vouch for its truth. For my own contemporaries
are witnesses fully acquainted with the incidents described and
will pass on to future ages an incontrovertible conviction that
these things have been faithfully recorded.

And yet there was something else which, when I was all agog
to get to work on this account, again and again held me back
for weeks on end. For I inclined to the view that the happiness
of those of future generations would be endangered by my
revelations, since it will be most advantageous that the deeds
of blackest dye shall if possible be unknown to future times,
rather than that they should come to the ears of tyrants as an
example to be imitated. For most rulers invariably, through
sheer ignorance, slip readily into imitation of their predecessors'
vices, and it is to the misdeeds of earlier rulers that they
invariably find it easier and less troublesome to turn. But later
on I was encouraged to write the narrative of these events by
this reflection – it will surely be evident to those tyrants of
the future that the penalty for their misdeeds is almost certain
to overtake them, just as it fell upon the persons described
here. Then again, their own conduct and character will in turn
be recorded for all time, and that will perhaps make them
less ready to transgress. For how could the licentious life of
Semiramis or the dementia of Sardanapaulus and Nero have
been known to anyone in later days if contemporary historians
had not left these things on record? Apart from this, those who
in the future, if it so happens, are similarly ill used at the hands
of tyrants will not find this record altogether useless; for it is
always comforting for those in distress to know that they are
not the only ones on whom these blows have fallen. For these
reasons, then, I shall proceed to recount all the wicked deeds
committed by Belisarius first, and then I shall reveal all the
wicked deeds committed by Justinian and Theodora.

[margin note, handwritten:] moral concerns of reading past

PART I

THE TYRANNY OF WOMEN

Belisarius was married to a woman of whom I had something to say in the preceding books.[2] Her father and grandfather were charioteers who had displayed their skill in both Byzantium and Thessalonica; her mother was one of the theatre tarts. She herself in her early years had lived a profligate kind of life and had thrown off all moral restraint; she had been continually in the company of her father's magic-mongering friends and had learnt the arts essential to her trade. Later when with all due ceremony she married Belisarius, she had already given birth to one child after another. So it was already her intention to be unfaithful from the start, but she took great care to conceal this business, not because her own conduct gave her any qualms, or because she stood in any fear of her spouse – she never felt the slightest shame for any action whatever, and thanks to her regular use of magic she had her husband wrapped round her little finger – but because she dreaded the vengeance of the Empress; for Theodora was only too ready to rage at her and bare her teeth in anger.[3] But by assisting her[4] in matters of exceptional importance, she quickly brought her to heel. The first step was to get rid of Silverius[5] by the means described by me in the following account;[6] the second was to ruin John the

2.   Antonina.
3.   Borrowed from Aristophanes' *Peace*.
4.   I.e. Theodora.
5.   Pope from 536 to 537.
6.   This may be a reference to an *Ecclesiastical History* that Procopius alludes to having envisaged writing but which he never wrote (see *Wars* 8.25.13). Alternatively, he may mean 'later in this volume': if so, he neglected to

Cappadocian, as described by me in my earlier writings.[7] The
way was now clear; her fears vanished and there was no further
concealment; she could commit every misdeed without the
slightest hesitation.

There was a certain lad from Thrace in the household of
Belisarius by the name of Theodosius, whose ancestral faith
was that of the so-called Eunomians.[8] On the eve of his voyage
to Libya, Belisarius washed this youth in the sacred bath, then
lifted him out in his arms, thereby making him the adopted son
of his wife and himself in accordance with the rules for adoption
observed by Christians. From that moment Antonina, as was
to be expected, loved Theodosius since the sacred word had
made him her son, and she watched over him with extreme care
and kept him under her wing. Then, a little while after, she fell
madly in love with him during this voyage and – surrendering
herself body and soul to her passion – threw off all fear and
respect for everything both divine and human, and had intercourse with him, at first in secret but finally before the very eyes
of the household servants and maids. For by now she was
helpless against this desire and unmistakably the slave of her
lust, so that she could no longer see any impediment to its
indulgence. Once, in Carthage, Belisarius caught them in the
very act, yet he swallowed his wife's lying explanation open-
mouthed. For though he had found them together in a basement
bedroom and was mad with rage, she did not flinch or disguise
what she had done but merely remarked, 'I came down here so
that the boy could help me bury the most precious of our spoils,
in case the Emperor should get to know about them.' This of
course was a mere excuse, but he seemed satisfied and let the
matter drop, although he could see full well that the thong that
held Theodosius' undergarments in place, covering his private
parts, had been unstrapped. For his passionate love for the

---

keep this promise, thus providing further evidence for the incomplete
nature of the text as it stands.

7. *Wars* 1.25.13.
8. Eunomius, a late fourth-century bishop of Cyzicus, held heretical views
    on the relationship between the persons of the Trinity.

[handwritten margin notes: wife = unfaithful / husband = moody/unpredict. / slave = honest]

woman compelled him to pretend that the evidence of his own eyes was utterly false.

Antonina's wantonness steadily increased till it had become an unspeakable scandal and everyone saw what was going on, but nobody said a word except a certain slave girl called Macedonia. In Syracuse, when Belisarius had conquered Sicily, this woman made her master swear the most dread oaths never to betray her to her mistress and then blurted out the whole story to him, corroborated by the testimony of two slave boys whose task was to look after the bedchamber. On hearing this, Belisarius ordered some of his retainers to deal with Theodosius once and for all.[9] Theodosius, however, heard of this in time and fled to Ephesus, for most of Belisarius' retainers, bearing in mind his swiftly changing moods, thought it more expedient to be in favour with the wife than the husband; so they betrayed the instructions then given to them regarding Theodosius. And when Constantine[10] saw how distressed Belisarius was by what had happened, he expressed his complete sympathy, adding the remark, 'If it were I, I should have destroyed the woman rather than the lad.' *[handwritten margin note: right?]* When this came to Antonina's ears, she kept her indignation against him secret, waiting for the right moment to display her hatred against him, for she was as a scorpion and concealed her feelings accordingly. A little while later, either by magic or by fawning, she convinced her husband that there was no truth in the girl's accusation, and he at once invited Theodosius to return, and agreed to hand over Macedonia and the slave boys to his wife. She first cut out the tongues of all three, we are told, then carved them up into little bits, which she dropped into sacks and then threw into the sea with utter nonchalance, assisted in all this unholy business by one of the household servants called Eugenius, the man who had been instrumental in the monstrous treatment of Silverius. A little while later, Belisarius was persuaded by his wife to kill Constantine too. For it was at this very time that the affair of Praesidius

9. These 'retainers' were probably Belisarius' *bucellarii*, or private men-at-arms, whom we know he took with him on campaign.
10. One of Belisarius' generals.

and the daggers took place, as has been described by me in the preceding account.[11] Constantine would have been acquitted, but Antonina would not relent until he had paid the penalty for the comment I have just mentioned. By his acquiescence Belisarius brought on himself the bitter hostility of the Emperor and of the leading Romans one and all.

So, then, did it come to pass. Theodosius, however, sent word that he would be unable to come to Italy, where Belisarius and Antonina were staying at the time, unless Photius was got out of the way.[12] For Photius was temperamentally quick to take offence if anyone else had more influence than he with any person. But in the case of Theodosius and his entourage, he had just cause for choking with rage: he himself, though he was a son, found himself counting for nothing, while his rival enjoyed great power and was becoming immensely wealthy. It is said that at Carthage and Ravenna he had purloined as much as one hundred *centenaria* of gold from the two palaces, which he was privileged to administer on his own responsibility and with full powers.[13] When Antonina learnt of Theodosius' refusal, she made persistent attempts to trap the boy and pursued him with murderous plots until she succeeded in forcing him to leave Italy and proceed to Byzantium, as he could no longer risk falling into her traps, and in persuading Theodosius to join her in Italy. There she enjoyed to the full both the company of her lover and the blindness of her husband, and a little later returned to Byzantium escorted by them both. In the capital Theodosius was in an agony of fear through the knowledge of his guilt, and his mind was perturbed. For he saw no possibility at all of averting suspicion, as he realized that Antonina could no longer keep her passion out of sight or give vent to it in secret, but rather, on the contrary, was perfectly happy to be an avowed adulteress and to be spoken of as such. So he again

11. *Wars* 6.8.1.
12. Son of Antonina by a previous partner.
13. A *centenaria* consisted of a hundred pounds' weight of gold, or 7,200 gold coins (*solidi*). By the end of the sixth century, one gold coin might have represented an entire year's salary to an indentured labourer on a great estate.

[handwritten margin notes: Theodosius keeps trying to leave, how much deception? she thought he really left?]

betook himself off to Ephesus and, adopting the customary tonsure, had himself enrolled amongst the 'monks', as they are called. At this Antonina became completely demented, and, changing her dress and her whole manner of life to the style of those in mourning, she wandered continually about the house, wailing, shrieking and lamenting even in the presence of her husband. What a good thing had been lost to her life; how faithful; how charming; how sweet-natured; how full of energy![14] Finally she even dragged her husband into these lamentations and made him join in. Anyway, the unfortunate man began weeping and crying aloud for his beloved Theodosius. Later he even approached the Emperor, appealing both to him and to the Empress, until he persuaded them to fetch Theodosius back, as he was indispensable to his household and always would be. Theodosius, however, flatly refused to leave Ephesus, insisting that he was determined to give unswerving obedience to the monastic discipline. This was a downright lie: the moment Belisarius left Byzantium, he planned to join Antonina surreptitiously. And join her he did.

[2] For very soon Belisarius, accompanied by Photius, was on his way to resume hostilities against Chosroes.[15] But Antonina stayed behind, a thing she had never done before: to prevent her husband from being alone and coming to his senses, and from treating her magic with contempt and seeing her for what she was, it was her invariable custom to accompany him to all parts of the world. And in order that Theodosius might be able to resume his association with her, she was impatient to get Photius out of the way. To this end she urged some of her husband's retainers to torment and insult him continually, never missing an opportunity, while she herself wrote almost every day, pouring out slanders in an endless stream and making the boy the target for every weapon. Under this treatment Photius perforce resolved to use slander against his mother, and when a man arrived from Byzantium with the news that Theodosius was secretly staying with Antonina, he at once took

14. Clearly a sexual innuendo.
15. Chosroes (Khusro) I was Shah of Persia from 531 to 579.

him into Belisarius' presence, adjuring him to tell the whole story.

When Belisarius learned the truth, he was beside himself with fury, and prostrated himself before Photius' feet and implored the boy to avenge him, monstrously ill used as he was by those from whom he least expected it. 'My most dear boy,' he cried, 'you have no idea what your father was like; for you were only a babe in arms when he departed this life, leaving you nothing at all; he was not overblessed with this world's goods. It was I who brought you up, though I am only your stepfather: now you have reached an age when it is your duty to defend me to the utmost if I am wronged; and you have risen to the rank of consul and have amassed so much wealth that I might justly be called, and indeed might be, my noble boy, your father and your mother and every other kinsman. For it is not by blood but by actions that people habitually measure their affection for one another. The time has come when you must no longer allow me, besides the wrecking of my home, to be stripped as well of possessions on so vast a scale, or your own mother to bring upon herself universal and utter contempt. And remember that the sins of women do not fall on their husbands only: they do still more damage to their children, whose misfortune it will almost certainly be to incur a reputation for having a natural resemblance in character to their mothers. You must realize too that this is the position with me: I love my wife dearly, and if I get the chance to give the wrecker of my home his deserts I shall do her no harm; but while Theodosius lives I can never forgive her for that of which she is accused.'

In reply to this Photius agreed to give all the help he could, though he was afraid it might cost him dear: he had precious little confidence in his stepfather's swiftly changing moods towards his wife, for a great many things worried him, especially what had happened to Macedonia. In view of this, the two swore to each other the most dread oaths that are in use among the Christians and are recognized as such, that they would never betray each other, even in situations of the most desperate danger. To make the attempt there and then struck them as inadvisable, but when Antonina arrived from Byzantium and

like war at home, on specific people

Theodosius went to Ephesus, that would be the moment for Photius to appear at Ephesus and take possession both of Theodosius and of the money with the minimum of trouble. Now at this very time when they had launched their all-out attack on Persian territory, the incident involving John the Cappadocian happened to be taking place in Byzantium, as I explained in the preceding narrative.[16] In that account, I confess, fear led me to suppress one fact. The deception of John and his daughter by Antonina was no casual occurrence: it was backed by a multitude of oaths, the most terrible form of declaration in Christian eyes, assuring them that no treachery was purposed towards them. When her object had been achieved and she felt much more secure in the affections of the Empress, she dispatched Theodosius to Ephesus, while she herself, anticipating no difficulty, set out for the East. Belisarius had just captured the fortress of Sisauranon when someone informed him of her imminent arrival. He instantly dismissed everything else from his mind and withdrew his forces. It happened that, as I made clear in my earlier account, certain other events which had taken place in the Roman camp disposed him to retreat at this time. But the information now received induced him to take this step much more precipitately. As I stated, however, at the start of this book, at that time I judged it too dangerous to disclose all the reasons for what had occurred.

The result of this move was that an accusation was levelled at Belisarius by Romans everywhere of having sacrificed the most vital interests of the state to his own domestic concerns. For at the start he had been so incapacitated by his wife's waywardness that he positively refused to go thus far beyond the bounds of the Roman Empire, determined as he was that the moment he learnt that his wife had arrived from Byzantium he must be able to turn back and catch and punish her there and then. For this reason he ordered Arethas and his men to cross the River Tigris,[17] and they, having accomplished nothing worthy of mention, departed for home, while he himself was

16. *Wars* 2.19.24.
17. Arethas (Al-Harith) was 'phylarch', or King, of the Ghassan – Byzantium's Arab clients along the Empire's desert frontier.

careful not to go even a day's march beyond the Roman frontier. The fortress of Sisauranon, even for a lightly equipped traveller, is certainly more than a day's journey from the limits of Roman territory if he goes via the city of Nisibis, but there is another route which is only half as long. And yet if he had been prepared from the first to cross the Tigris with his entire army, I have no doubt that he would have despoiled all the districts of Assyria, gone right on to the city of Ctesiphon without meeting any resistance at all, freed the prisoners from Antioch and any other Romans who happened to be there, and then returned safely to the fatherland.[18] Then again it was mainly his fault that Chosroes met no real opposition on the way back from Colchis. How this happened I will explain forthwith.

sidestep

When Chosroes, son of Cabades, invaded the territory of Colchis and won the successes which I recorded earlier,[19] including the capture of Petra, the Persian army suffered heavy casualties both in the actual fighting and in negotiating the difficult terrain. As I have pointed out, roads are almost non-existent in Lazica, and precipices abound on every side.[20] As if that was not enough, an epidemic swept through the army and most of the soldiers died, while many of the survivors perished for want of necessities. At this crisis too, persons arriving there from Persia brought the news that Belisarius had defeated Nabedes in battle near the city of Nisibis and was now advancing; that he had stormed Sisauranon and taken Bleschames prisoner with 800 Persian cavalry; that he had dispatched another Roman force under Arethas the Saracen commander; and that this force had crossed the Tigris and plundered all the villages there, which until then had remained unravaged. It happened also that Chosroes had sent a column of Huns against the Armenians who were Roman subjects, in the hope that the Romans in that locality would be so busy dealing with this threat that they would be oblivious to events in Lazica. Other messengers now brought word that these barbarians had been

---

18. Ctesiphon was the capital of the Sasanian Empire; Antioch had been sacked by the Persians in 540.

19. *Wars* 2.24.

20. *Wars* 2.29.24–5.

intercepted by Valerian and his Romans; they had joined battle *how* *wild* with them and had been severely worsted in the encounter, the column being almost wiped out. *Procopius know this?*

When the Persians heard these things, and partly by virtue of the untold misery they had suffered in Lazica, as also their apprehensiveness lest during their retreat they should run into some enemy force in the narrow defiles and dense thickets, and in their sorry disarray be utterly destroyed, and also because they had become alarmed by the danger to their wives and children and to their homeland, every honest man in the Persian army began to protest vehemently to Chosroes, accusing him, in violation of both his own oaths and the laws held in common by all mankind, of invading Roman territory entirely without provocation whilst a truce was in place and of wronging by his aggression an ancient state that was superior to all others in dignity, and that could not be overcome in war. They were on the verge of mutiny. Chosroes, seriously alarmed, attempted to cure the distemper with the following remedy. He read aloud to them a letter which the Empress happened to have written to Zaberganes a little while before. The contents were as follows:

What an impression you made on me, Zaberganes, by your evident regard for our interests, you saw for yourself a little while back, when you came as an ambassador to our court. My high opinion of you would be confirmed if you were to induce the Emperor Chosroes to pursue a peaceful policy towards our state. In that case, I can guarantee that you will reap a handsome reward from my husband, who would not think of taking any action whatever without my approval. *disregard true offer from Theodora*

When Chosroes had read this aloud, he took to task any of the Persian nobles who imagined that any state worth the name was run by a woman. He managed thus to stem the violence of the men's hostility, but even so he was very apprehensive as he marched away, fully expecting to find his route blocked by the forces of Belisarius. Not a single foe, however, appeared on his path, and to his great relief he got back safely to his own domain.

[3] On reaching Roman territory, Belisarius found that his wife had arrived from Byzantium. He kept her under guard in disgrace and made repeated moves to get rid of her altogether. But he always relented, overcome, it seems to me, by fiery passion. Rumour has it that his wife used magic arts to enslave him, instantly destroying his resolution. Meanwhile Photius set off posthaste for Ephesus, taking with him one of the eunuchs, Calligonus by name, who served as procurer for his mistress. He had put the man in fetters, and on the journey he tortured him until he disclosed all of Antonina's secrets. Theodosius, forewarned, took sanctuary in the Church of John the Apostle, the most sacred shrine in Ephesus and one held in special honour. But Andrew, the Archpriest of Ephesus, accepted a bribe and handed him over to his pursuer.

Meanwhile Theodora, who had heard all that had befallen Antonina and was anxious for her safety, ordered Belisarius to bring her to Byzantium. Photius on learning this sent Theodosius into Cilicia, where the guards and armed retainers happened to be quartered for the winter, instructing the escort to convey the prisoner with the utmost stealth, and on arrival in Cilicia to keep him in an absolutely safe place of confinement, giving no one a chance to discover his whereabouts. He himself, accompanied by Calligonus, took Theodosius' money, amounting to a very considerable sum, to Byzantium. There the Empress was demonstrating to the world that she knew how to repay bloody favours with bigger and more polluted gifts. Antonina had recently entrapped a single enemy, the Cappadocian, and betrayed him to Theodora: Theodora handed over a small army of men to Antonina and without proferring a charge brought them to destruction. Some of the close friends of Belisarius and Photius she subjected to physical tortures, even though she had nothing against them except their friendship with these two men, and she disposed of them in such a way that even now we do not know what happened to them in the end. Others too she charged with the same offence and sentenced to banishment. One of the men who had accompanied Photius to Ephesus, Theodosius by name, though he had been honoured with membership of the Senate, she deprived of his property and threw into a dungeon, where he was forced to stand in pitch darkness, his neck tied to a manger with a noose so small that it was always pulled tight round his throat and never for a moment loosened. And so the poor fellow stood continuously at this manger, eating and sleeping, and performing all other natural functions; he resembled an ass in every particular short of braying. Four months, no less, he passed in this sort of existence, until he was overcome by sick melancholy and went stark mad; then at last he was released from his prison and promptly died.

Theodora also compelled Belisarius, much against his inclination, to lay aside his quarrel with his wife Antonina. Photius she subjected to one servile torture after another, tearing the flesh off his back and shoulders with merciless flogging, insisting that he should disclose the whereabouts of Theodosius and the procurer. But Photius, despite the torment that he was enduring, was determined to keep his sworn word, though he was of feeble constitution and had been dissolute in his youth, and had always attended to his physical comfort with the greatest care, while rough treatment and hardship were unknown to him. Anyway, Photius gave away none of Belisarius' secrets; later, however, all the facts hitherto concealed came to light. The Empress also found Calligonus there and passed him over to Antonina.

Next she summoned Theodosius to Byzantium, and when he arrived she for the moment concealed him in the Palace: next day she sent for Antonina and said, 'Dearest Patrician: a pearl fell into my hands yesterday, the most beautiful that has ever been seen. If you wish, I shall not grudge you the sight of it but will show it to you.' Antonina, who did not grasp the purport of all this, begged and besought the Empress to show her the pearl. Whereupon Theodosius was produced from the chamber of one of the eunuchs and shown to her. Antonina was so overcome with joy that at first she was too delighted to say a word; then she acknowledged that Theodora had indeed showered favours upon her, and hailed her as Saviour and Benefactress and Mistress. This Theodosius the Empress detained in the Palace, surrounding him with luxury and pleasures of every kind, and swearing that she would make him a general in the Roman army in the near future. But justice of a sort forestalled her: he had an attack of dysentery, and that was the end of him.

Now Theodora had some secret little rooms completely hidden from view, pitch-dark and isolated, where night and day were indistinguishable. There she imprisoned Photius and kept him under guard for a long time. From this prison he had the extraordinary luck to escape twice over and get away. The first time he took refuge in the Church of the Mother of God, which the Byzantines consider Most Holy – the name that was actually given to it – and sat down before the holy table as a suppliant. From there Theodora removed him by brute force and sent him back to prison. The second time he went to the sanctuary of Sophia,[21] and before anyone could stop him he actually sat down in the divine receptacle itself, which the Christians at all times reverence more than anything else. But even from there the woman was able to drag him: there was not one inviolable spot that remained beyond her reach, and in her eyes violence done to sacred things of any and every kind was nothing at all. And like the common people the Christian priests were so terrified of her that they left the way clear and allowed her to do as she liked. So it was that Photius spent no less than three years in this kind of existence, but afterwards the prophet Zachariah stood over him in a dream and, it is said, commanded him to flee, solemnly promising to assist him in this endeavour. Convinced by this vision, he broke out of his prison and made his way to Jerusalem without being caught; for though thousands were on the lookout for him, not a single person recognized him even after meeting him face to face. In Jerusalem he adopted the tonsure and arrayed himself in the habit of the 'monks', as they are called, managing thus to escape Theodora's vengeance.

Belisarius, on the other hand, had paid no regard to his oath and had chosen to give no help at all to his stepson, although he was being treated in the abominable way that I have

21. Hagia Sophia, or the Church of 'Holy Wisdom', in Constantinople.

[handwritten: tying personal promises/loyalty to outcomes/fate]

described. So it is not surprising that in all his subsequent undertakings he found the hand of God against him. For no sooner had he been dispatched against Chosroes and his Persians, who had for the third time invaded Roman territory, than he laid himself open to a charge of cowardice. He did indeed appear to have won a notable success in that he had shaken off war from that region. But when Chosroes crossed the River Euphrates, captured the teeming city of Callinicum without meeting any resistance, and enslaved tens of thousands of Romans, Belisarius did not bother even to pursue the army, leaving people to think that one of two things must be true: he had hung back either through wilful neglect of his duty or through sheer cowardice.

[4] It was not long before Belisarius suffered another blow. The plague that I described in the previous narrative was rampaging through the population of Byzantium.[22] Among those struck was the Emperor Justinian, who became very ill indeed; it was even stated that he was dead. The story was spread about by rumour and carried right to the Roman camp. There some of the officers declared that if the Romans in Byzantium set up someone else of his sort as Emperor over them, they would never put up with it. But the unexpected happened, and before long the Emperor recovered; thereupon the officers of the army flung accusations at each other. Peter the general and John, nicknamed 'The Guzzler', insisted that they had heard Belisarius and Bouzes talking in the way I have just mentioned. These criticisms, the Empress Theodora alleged, had been directed by their authors against herself, and she could not contain her indignation. She instantly recalled them all to Byzantium and held an enquiry into the report. Then without notice she summoned Bouzes to her private apartment as if to consult him on some matter of the utmost importance.

[handwritten: now Theodora is making changes, operating on rumor]

There was a system of cellars beneath the Palace, secure and labyrinthine, and suggestive of Tartarus itself. In these she habitually kept locked up any who had incurred her displeasure. Into this hole Bouzes was flung in his turn, and there, though

22. *Wars* 2.22.

the descendant of consuls, he remained, forever oblivious to the passage of time. For as he sat in darkness he could not himself make out whether it was day or night, and he was never allowed to speak to anyone else. The man who tossed him his daily ration of food met him as beast meets beast, neither saying a word. Everyone took it for granted that he had died at once, but to mention his name or to say a word about him was more than anyone dared to do. Two years and four months later, Theodora took pity on her prisoner and set him free. Everybody stared at him as if he had come back from the dead. For the rest of his life the unfortunate man suffered from bad eyesight, and his general health was very feeble.

Such was the treatment meted out to Bouzes. Belisarius, although none of the charges was brought home to him, was at the instigation of the Empress deprived by the Emperor of the command which he held and replaced by Martin as General of the East. Belisarius' guards and men-at-arms, together with those of his personal retainers who were trained fighting men, were, on the Emperor's orders, to be divided up between some of the officers and Palace eunuchs. These drew lots for them and shared them, arms and all, among themselves, as each man happened to be lucky. Many of his friends and other old helpers were forbidden to associate with Belisarius any more. A pitiful sight and an incredible spectacle, Belisarius went about as a private citizen in Byzantium, almost alone, always gloomy and melancholy, in continual fear of death by a murderer's hand. Learning that he had accumulated great wealth in the East, the Empress sent one of the Palace eunuchs to bring it all to her.

Antonina, as I have said, had fallen out with her husband but was an inseparable friend of the Empress because she had recently contrived to ruin John the Cappadocian. So the Empress, determined to gratify Antonina, did all in her power to make it seem that it was thanks to his wife's intercessions that the husband had been spared and saved from his calamitous position, and to arrange matters so that Antonina should not only be completely reconciled with her unfortunate husband but should unmistakably be his rescuer as if she had saved a prisoner of war. It happened in this way. Early one morning

[handwritten: husband + wife as independent units (not on same side)]

Belisarius came to the Palace, escorted as usual by a few poor specimens of humanity. He found their majesties anything but friendly and into the bargain was grossly insulted there by some vulgar scoundrels. It was late in the evening when he set off for home, and on the way back he repeatedly turned round and looked in every possible direction from which he might see his would-be murderers coming towards him. In the grip of this terror, he went upstairs to his bedroom and sat down on the bed alone, thinking not one worthy thought nor even cognisant of the fact that he had ever been a man. The sweat ran down his face unceasingly; his head swam; his whole body trembled in an agony of despair, tormented as he was by slavish fears and craven anxieties utterly unworthy of a man.

Antonina, as if she was quite unaware of what was afoot and had no inkling of anything that was to happen, was walking endlessly about the room to relieve an alleged attack of heartburn, for they still eyed each other suspiciously. *[handwritten: they still live together..]* Meanwhile a man called Quadratus arrived from the Palace when it was already dark, passed through the outer gateway and appeared without warning outside the door of the men's apartments, announcing that the Empress had sent him there. When Belisarius heard this, he drew up his hands and feet on the bed and lay motionless on his back, convinced that his time had come, so completely had every spark of manhood deserted him. Without waiting to get near him, Quadratus held up a letter from the Empress for him to see. It read as follows:

> How you have behaved towards us, noble sir, you know only too well. But I personally owe so much to your wife that for her sake I have resolved to dismiss all the charges against you, making her a present of your life. So from now on you need have no fear for either your life or your money. How you regard your wife your future conduct will show us.

When Belisarius had read the letter through, he was beside himself with joy and longed at the same time to show there and then how he felt. So he sprang up at once, threw himself on his face at his wife's feet and flung his arms round both her knees.

Then, raining kisses on each ankle in turn, he declared that he owed his life entirely to her and swore that henceforth he would be her faithful slave, not her husband. Of his money the Empress gave thirty *centenaria* of gold to the Emperor and returned the remnant to Belisarius.

Such was the downfall of the general Belisarius, to whom Fortune a little while before had presented Gelimer and Vittigis as prisoners of war.[23] But for a long time both Justinian and Theodora had been bitterly jealous of the man's wealth, as it was too great, and more suited to the court of an Emperor. They maintained that he had spirited away the bulk of the money in the public treasuries of Gelimer and Vittigis, handing over a tiny and quite negligible fraction of it to the Emperor. But the toils Belisarius had undergone and the execration they would bring upon themselves could not be disregarded; nor could they devise any convincing excuse for taking action against him. So they bided their time. But now the Empress had caught him in a state of abject terror and completely cowed, a single stroke sufficed to make her mistress of his entire property. For a relationship by marriage was promptly established between them by the union of Joannina, the only child of Belisarius, with Anastasius, the son of the Empress's daughter. Belisarius now asked to be restored to his proper position and appointed Commander-in-Chief in the East, so that he could again lead the Roman army against Chosroes and the Persians. But Antonina would not hear of it: in that part of the world, she insisted, she had been grossly insulted by him, and he should never see it again.

And so, for this reason, Belisarius was appointed Commander of the Imperial Grooms, and for the second time he set out for Italy, after giving the Emperor an undertaking, it is said, that he would never ask him for money during the campaign but would himself pay for all the necessary equipment out of his own pocket. It was universally surmised that Belisarius settled the problem of his wife in this way, and gave the Emperor

23. Kings respectively of the Vandal Kingdom of Africa and the Ostrogothic Kingdom of Italy.

was Procopius Christian?

the undertaking described above regarding the forthcoming campaign, simply with the object of getting away from life in Byzantium; and that the moment he found himself outside the city walls he would instantly resort to arms and plunge into some gallant and heroic enterprise in order to score off his wife and those who had humiliated him. Belisarius, however, paid no heed to anything that had happened: completely oblivious and indifferent to the oaths which he had sworn to Photius and all his most intimate friends, he went where his wife directed him, for he was hopelessly in love with her, though she was already a woman of sixty.

which were just to not betray Photius (p 8)

But when he arrived in Italy, there was not a single day when things went right for him, because the hand of God was unmistakably against him. At first, it is true, the plans which in the circumstances he devised for dealing with Theodahad and Vittigis, though apparently unsuited to his purpose, for the most part brought about the desired result; but in the later stages, despite the reputation he won for having planned his campaign on sound lines as a result of the experience gained in dealing with the problems of this war, his ill success in the sequel was for the most part put down to apparent errors of judgement. So true is it that it is not our own devices that control our lives but the power of God – although men are wont to call this Fortune, simply because we do not know what makes events follow the course we see them follow. When there seems to be no reason for a thing, it is almost inevitably put down to Fortune. But let each man form an opinion on such matters as he chooses.

[5] So it was that, after coming to Italy a second time, Belisarius returned home utterly discredited. For, as described by me in the previous account,[24] in spite of five years' effort he never once succeeded in disembarking on any part of the coast, unless there was a fortress handy: the whole of that time he sailed about, trying one landing place after another. Totila[25] was desperate to catch him outside a protecting wall, but he failed to

24. *Wars* 7.25.1.
25. A Goth who was elected King in 541 and overran most of Italy but in 552 was defeated and killed by Narses.

make contact, as Belisarius himself and the entire Roman army were in the grip of panic, with the result that he not only failed to recover any of what had been lost but actually lost Rome as well, and very nearly everything else. At the same time he devoted himself heart and soul to the pursuit of wealth and the unlimited acquisition of illicit gain, on the plea that he had not received a penny from the Emperor. In fact, he plundered indiscriminately nearly all the Italians who lived at Ravenna or in Sicily and anyone else he could reach, pretending that he was making them pay the penalty for their misdeeds. Thus he even went for Herodian,[26] demanding money from him and using every possible means to terrorize him. This so infuriated Herodian that he turned his back on the Roman army and at once put himself, the units under his command and the town of Spolitium in the hands of Totila and the Goths. And how Belisarius came to quarrel with Vitalian's nephew John, thereby doing untold damage to the Roman cause, is the next question that I must answer.

Such savage enmity against Germanus had the Empress conceived – enmity of which she made no secret at all – that although he was the Emperor's nephew no one dared marry into his family, and his sons remained single until their best years were past them. His daughter Justina too, though she was a mature woman of eighteen, was still without a bridegroom. Consequently when John was dispatched by Belisarius on an errand to Byzantium, Germanus was compelled to negotiate with him on the subject of a marriage with her, in spite of the fact that John's rank was far inferior to his own. As the suggestion appealed to them both, they agreed to bind each other by the most dread oaths that they would do everything in their power to effect the proposed union, for each of them profoundly distrusted the other, the one being aware that he was reaching far beyond his rank, the other having no hope of a son-in-law.

This was more than the Empress could bear. Putting all her scruples aside, she went for them both with every available

26. A Roman commander.

vision of dastardly grandmas

weapon and without hesitation in her determination to bring their plans to nothing. When all her efforts at intimidation produced no effect on either of them, she announced in so many words that she would destroy John. In consequence, when John was again dispatched to Italy, he dared not go anywhere near Belisarius for fear of Antonina's machinations until that lady was safely back in Byzantium. For there was every reason to suspect that the Empress had entrusted her with the task of arranging his murder, and as John weighed Antonina's character and reminded himself that Belisarius let his wife have her own way in everything, he was seized with uncontrollable fear. This situation brought low the fortunes of the Romans, already teetering on their last legs.

This, then, is how the Gothic War went for Belisarius. Despairing of success, he appealed to the Emperor for permission to leave Italy forthwith. When he learnt that Justinian was agreeable to his requests he was delighted and, bidding farewell to the Roman army and to the Italians, set off immediately for home, leaving most of the fortresses in the hands of the enemy and the city of Perusia in the grip of a bitter siege. Indeed, before his journey was even completed, the city was taken by storm and experienced every horror imaginable, as has been described by me previously.[27] At the same time a heavy blow fell upon his own household, as we shall see next.

Belisarius = unresponsive

The Empress Theodora, impatient to secure the betrothal of Belisarius' daughter to her own grandson, wrote letter after letter to the girl's parents, worrying them to death. They, in their anxiety to prevent the alliance, sought to postpone the marriage until they themselves returned, and when summoned to Byzantium by the Empress pleaded that they could not leave Italy just then. But she had set her heart on making her grandson master of Belisarius' wealth, knowing that it would all go to the girl, as Belisarius had no other child. She put no trust, however, in the intentions of Antonina and was afraid that when she herself departed from the scene, Antonina would show no loyalty towards the imperial house – although

so much distrust + deception!

27. *Wars* 7.35.2.

Theodora had treated her so generously when she was in great difficulties – but would tear up the contract. And so, in defiance of all morality, she made the underage girl live with the boy in unlawful union. It is said that by secret pressure she actually forced her, though most unwilling, to have intercourse with him and – when in this way the girl had lost her virginity – arranged for her to marry him, for fear the Emperor might put a stop to her little game. However, when the deed was done, a burning love for each other took possession of Anastasius and his child bride, and they spent eight whole months together in blissful union.

But when death removed the Empress, Antonina came to Byzantium and, wilfully oblivious of the favours Theodora had so recently bestowed on her, paid no regard at all to the fact that if she married the girl to anyone else, her previous relationship would be regarded as an act of prostitution. She had no use for Theodora's offspring as son-in-law, and although the girl was unwilling in the extreme she compelled her to part from the man she adored. By this action she won a universal reputation for utter heartlessness, and yet when her husband arrived she had no difficulty at all in persuading him to share the responsibility with her for this abominable outrage.

This, then, was the moment when the man's character was laid bare for all to see. It is true that when on an earlier occasion he had given his sworn word to Photius and some of his closest friends, and then had shamelessly broken it, he had been forgiven by everyone. For the cause of his faithlessness, they suspected, was not his subservience to his wife but fear of the Empress. But when, as I mentioned, death removed Theodora, he paid no regard either to Photius or to any of those nearest to him but allowed it to be seen that his wife was mistress over him, and Caligonus her procurer was master. Then at last he was repudiated by everyone, was made the target of endless gossip and was dismissed with contempt as a hopeless fool. Such then is the record – unvarnished and essentially correct – of the misdeeds of Belisarius.

Let us now turn to those misdeeds committed in Libya by Sergius, son of Bacchus, of which I gave an adequate account in the appropriate place, showing that he did more than anyone to destroy Roman authority in that region,[28] for he not only treated with contempt the oaths which he had sworn on the Gospels to the Leuathae but even put the eighty ambassadors to death without the slightest pretext. Only one addition need now be made to my account, namely that these men had no sinister motive in coming to Sergius, and Sergius had no excuse for suspecting them: he pledged his word to them, invited them to dinner and put them to death in the most dastardly manner. It was this outrage that brought about the destruction of Solomon and the Roman army, and of all the Libyans; for on his account, especially after the death of Solomon which I recorded earlier, not an officer nor an ordinary soldier was prepared for the hazards of war. Worst of all, John son of Sisinniolus was so furious with him that he kept clear of all fighting until Areobindus arrived in Libya. For Sergius was effeminate and unwarlike, in character and development quite immature, a helpless slave to envy and boastfulness towards everyone, ostentatious in his way of life and blown up with pride. But, as it happened, he had become a suitor for the grand-daughter of Antonina, Belisarius' wife, so the Empress absolutely declined to punish him in any way or to deprive him of his command, although she saw that the ruin of Libya was proceeding apace; with the full approval of the Emperor she even allowed Sergius' brother Solomon, the murderer of Pegasius, to go scot-free. How this happened I will speedily make clear.

When Pegasius had ransomed Solomon from the Leuathae and the tribe had gone back home, Solomon, along with Pegasius his ransomer and a handful of soldiers, set out for Carthage. On the way Pegasius caught Solomon committing an offence of some sort and remarked with considerable emphasis that he ought not to forget how, a short time before, God had rescued him from the enemy. Solomon, thinking that he had been sneered at for letting himself be taken a prisoner, lost his temper and killed Pegasius on the spot – a poor return for the

28. *Wars* 4.31.1.

man who had saved him. When Solomon arrived in Byzantium, the Emperor acquitted him of the murder on the grounds that he had executed a traitor to the Roman Empire. He furthermore gave him a letter ensuring his immunity from any proceedings in this matter. Having thus escaped punishment, Solomon went off in great glee to the East, to visit his birthplace and his family at home. But punishment at the hand of God overtook him on the way and removed him from human sight. So much for Solomon and Pegasius.

covers the minor couple that outlive J+T first

PART II
JUSTINIAN AND THEODORA

[6] What sort of people Justinian and Theodora were and how it came about that they destroyed the fortunes of the Roman Empire I shall now proceed to tell. When Leo occupied the imperial throne of Byzantium,[29] three peasant lads of Illyrian origin – Zimarchus, Dityvistus and Justin (who came from Vederiana) – men who at home had to contend ceaselessly with conditions of grinding poverty and all that went with it, set out to join the army in an effort to better their lot. They covered the whole distance to Byzantium on foot, carrying on their shoulders cloaks in which on their arrival they had nothing but a few dry biscuits which they had put there before they had left home. Their names were entered on the muster roll, and the Emperor picked them out to serve in the Palace guard as they were men of exceptional physique.

Some time later, when Anastasius had succeeded to the imperial power,[30] he was involved in a war with the Isaurians, who had taken up arms against him. He sent an army of considerable size to deal with them, the commander being John the Hunchback. This John had locked Justin up in prison because of some misdemeanour, intending to dispatch him on the following day. This he would have done but for a dream-vision which came to him in time to prevent it. The general said that in a dream he was confronted by a being of colossal size, too powerful in every way to be taken for a man. This being ordered him to release the man whom he had that day imprisoned: he

29. Leo I (457–74).
30. Anastasius (491–518).

himself on waking from sleep dismissed the vision from his mind. But when the next night came, he dreamt that he again heard the same words as before but remained just as unwilling to carry out the order. Then for the third time the vision stood over him, threatening total ruin unless he did as he was told and adding that one day he would be in a great rage, and then he would need this man and his family.

This occurrence enabled Justin to survive his immediate danger, and as time went on he acquired great power. The Emperor Anastasius gave him command of the Palace guards, and when he himself passed away, Justin on the strength of this command succeeded to the throne, though he was by now a doddering old man, totally illiterate – in popular parlance, he didn't know his ABC – an unheard of thing amongst the Romans. It was the invariable custom that the Emperor should append his own signature to all documents embodying decrees defined by him. Justin, however, was incapable of either drafting his own decrees or taking an intelligent interest in the measures contemplated: the official whose luck it was to be his chief adviser – a man called Proclus, who held the rank of Quaestor, as it is called – used to decide all measures as he himself thought fit. But to secure authority for these in the Emperor's own handwriting, the men responsible for this business proceeded as follows. On a short strip of polished wood they cut a stencil in the shape of four letters spelling the Latin for *I HAVE READ*.[31] Then they used to dip a pen in the special ink reserved for emperors and place it in the hands of the Emperor Justin. Next they took the strip of wood I have described and laid it on the document, grasped the Emperor's hand and, while he held the pen, guided it along the pattern of the four letters, taking it round all the bends cut in the wooden stencil. Then away they went, carrying the Emperor's writing, such as it was.

That was the kind of Emperor the Romans had in Justin. He was married to a woman called Lupicina, a slave and barbarian who had previously been purchased by another man and had

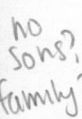
(handwritten margin note: no sons? family?)

31. *LEGI.*

become his concubine. But in the evening of her days she became joint ruler with Justin of the Roman Empire. Justin was not capable of doing any harm to his subjects or any good either. He was uncouth in the extreme, utterly inarticulate and incredibly boorish. His nephew Justinian, though still quite young, used to manage all the affairs of state, and he brought on the Romans disasters which surely surpassed both in gravity and in number all that had ever been heard of at any period of history. For without the slightest hesitation he used to embark on the inexcusable murdering of his fellow-men and the plundering of other people's property, and it did not matter to him how many thousands lost their lives, although they had given him no provocation whatever. The maintenance of established institutions meant nothing to him: endless innovations were his constant preoccupation. In a word, he was a great destroyer of well-established institutions.

Now, the plague, which was described by me in my earlier writings, fell upon the whole world, yet just as many people escaped as had the misfortune to succumb – either because they escaped the infection altogether, or because they got over it if they happened to be infected.[32] But this man not a single person in the whole Roman Empire could escape: like any other visitation from heaven falling on the entire human race, he left no one completely untouched. Some he killed without any justification; others he reduced to penury, making them even more wretched than those who had died. In fact, they begged him to put an end to their misery, by any death however painful. Some he deprived of their possessions and of life as well. But it gave him no satisfaction merely to ruin the Roman Empire: he insisted on making himself the master of Libya and Italy for the sole purpose of destroying their inhabitants along with those already subject to him. He had not been ten days in office before he executed Amantius, controller of the Palace eunuchs, with several others, for no reason at all, charging him with nothing more than an injudicious joke about John, the

---

32. Originating in Central Africa, the plague first reached the Empire via Egypt in 541 before spreading throughout the Mediterranean.

archpriest of the city. This outrage made him more feared than any man alive. His next step was to send for the pretender Vitalian, whose safety he had previously guaranteed by taking part with him in the Christian sacraments. But a little later Justinian took offence through groundless suspicion and put him to death in the Palace along with his closest friends without the slightest justification, making no attempt to honour his pledges, the most solemn imaginable.

[7] The people have long been divided into two factions, as I explained in my earlier account.[33] Justinian attached himself to one of them, the Blues, to whom he had already given enthusiastic support, and so contrived to produce universal chaos. By doing so he brought the Roman state to its knees. However, not all the Blues were prepared to follow the lead of Justinian, only the most militant of the factionalists. Yet even these, as things went from bad to worse, appeared to be the most self-disciplined of men, for the licence given them went far beyond the misdemeanours which they actually committed. Needless to say the Green factionalists did not stay quiet either: they too pursued an uninterrupted career of crime, as far as they were permitted, although at every moment one or other was paying the penalty. As a result they were constantly provoked to commit crimes far more audacious still; for when people are unfairly treated, they naturally turn to desperate courses. So now that he was fanning the flames and openly spurring on the Blues, the entire Roman Empire was shaken to the foundations as if an earthquake or deluge had struck it, or as if every city had fallen to the enemy. For everywhere there was utter chaos, and nothing was the same ever again: in the confusion that followed, the laws and the orderly structure of the state were turned upside down.

To begin with, the factionalists changed the style of their hair to a quite novel fashion, having it cut very differently from the other Romans. They did not touch the moustache or beard at all but were always anxious to let them grow as long as possible, like the Persians. But the hair on the front of the head they cut

33. *Wars* 1.24.2.

right back to the temples, allowing the growth behind to hang down to its full length in a disorderly mass, like the Massagetae do. This is why they sometimes called this the Hunnish look.[34] Then, as regards dress, they all thought it necessary to be luxuriously turned out, donning attire too ostentatious for their particular station. For they were in a position to obtain such garments at other people's expense. The part of the tunic covering their arms was drawn in very tight at the wrists, while from there to the shoulders it spread out to an enormous width. Whenever they waved their arms as they shouted in the theatre or the hippodrome and encouraged their favourites in the usual way, up in the air went this part of their tunics, giving silly people the notion that their bodies were so splendidly sturdy that they had to be covered with garments of this size: they did not realize that the transparency and emptiness of their attire served rather to show up their miserable physiques. Their capes and breeches too, and in most cases their shoes, were classed as Hunnish in name and fashion.

At first the great majority carried weapons at night quite openly, while in the daytime they concealed short two-edged swords along their thighs under their cloaks. They used to collect in gangs at nightfall and rob members of the upper class in the open forum or in narrow alleys, despoiling any they met of cloaks, belts, gold brooches and anything else they had with them. Some they thought it better to murder as well as rob, since dead men told no tales. These outrages caused universal indignation, especially among those Blues who were not militant factionalists, since they suffered as badly as the rest. Consequently from then on most people wore belts and brooches of bronze, and cloaks of much poorer quality than their station warranted, for fear that their love of the beautiful would cost them their lives, and even before sunset they hurried back home

34. The factionalists wore what in modern slang would be called 'mullets'. The long hair of the tribes of the Eurasian steppes was something of a preoccupation amongst Roman authors of a conservative mindset: Procopius' contemporary, the poet Corippus, describes an embassy of Avars that arrived at the court of Justin II as 'shabby with their snake-like hair'.

and got under cover. As this shocking state of affairs continued and no notice was taken of the offenders by the authorities in charge of the city, the audacity of these men increased by leaps and bounds. For when nothing is done to discourage wrongdoing, there is of course no limit to its growth: even when punishment does follow offences, it does not often put an end to them altogether: it is natural for most people to turn easily to wrongdoing.

This is how things went with the Blues. Of their opponents some came over to their faction through a desire to join in their criminal activities without paying any penalty, others took flight and slipped away to other lands; many who were caught in the city were put out of the way by their opponents or executed by the authorities. Many other young men poured into this organization: they had never before shown any interest in such things, but ambition for power and unrestrained licence attracted them to it. For there is not one revolting crime known to men which was not at that time committed and left unpunished. They began by destroying the partisans of the opposite faction, then went on to murder those who had given them no provocation whatever. Many also won them over with bribes, then implicated their own enemies; these the factionalists got rid of at once, labelling them Greens though they knew nothing at all about them. All this went on no longer in darkness or out of sight but at any moment of the day and in every part of the city, and the most eminent citizens as often as not were eyewitnesses to what was happening. There was no need to keep the crimes concealed, since the criminals were not troubled by any fear of punishment; in fact they were actually moved by a spirit of rivalry, so that they organized displays of brawn and toughness to show that with a single blow they could kill anyone they met unarmed, and no one now could expect to live much longer amid the dangers that daily threatened him. Constant fear made everyone expect that death was just round the corner: no place seemed safe, no time could guarantee security, since even in the most revered sanctuaries and at public festivals people were being senselessly murdered, and confidence in kith and kin was a thing of the past. For many perished through the machinations of their nearest relatives.

No inquiry, however, was held into the crimes committed: the blow invariably fell without warning, and the fallen had no one to avenge them. No law or contract retained any force on the secure basis of the established order, but everything turned to growing violence and confusion, and the government was indistinguishable from a tyranny – not, however, a stable tyranny but one that changed every day and was forever starting afresh. The decisions of the magistrates suggested the paralysis of fear – their minds were dominated by dread of a single man – and those who sat in judgement, when settling questions in dispute, based their verdicts not on their notions of what was just and lawful but on the relations, hostile or friendly, which each of the disputants had with the partisans. For any judge who disregarded their injunctions would pay the price with his life.

And many creditors were under irresistible pressure to return promissory notes to their debtors without recovering any of the debt, and many people to their chagrin had to free their household slaves, and it is said that a number of women were forced by their own slaves to yield to many acts most repugnant to them. And by now the sons of men in high positions, after associating with these young criminals, compelled their fathers to do a number of things they were most reluctant to do, particularly to hand over their money to them. Many unwilling boys, with the full knowledge of their fathers, were forced to have unholy intercourse with faction members, and women who were happily married suffered the same treatment. It is said that one woman, very elegantly attired, was travelling by boat with her husband to one of the suburbs on the mainland opposite, and during this crossing the partisans intercepted them, tore the lady from her husband's arms and carried her into their own boat. Before going on board with the young men, she whispered encouragement to her husband and told him to have no fear on her account: she would never submit to physical outrage. Then, while her husband was still watching her through his tears, she jumped overboard and from that moment was never seen again.

Such were the acts of violence of which the factionalists in Byzantium were guilty at that period. But these things caused less misery to the victims than the wrongs which the community suffered at Justinian's hands, because those whom miscreants have injured the most cruelly are relieved of most of the misery resulting from a disordered society by the constant expectation that the laws and the government will punish the offenders. For when people are confident of the future they find their present troubles more tolerable and easier to bear; but when they are subjected to violence by the state authorities they are naturally more distressed by the wrongs they have suffered, and fall into utter despair through the hopelessness of expecting justice. Justinian betrayed his subjects not only because he absolutely refused to uphold the victims of wrong, but because he was perfectly prepared to set himself up as the recognized champion of the factionalists; for he lavished great sums of money on these young men and kept many of them in his entourage, actually promoting some to magistracies and other official positions.

[8] Such, then, was the state of affairs in Byzantium and every other city. For like any other disease the infection that began in the capital rapidly spread all over the Roman Empire. The Emperor Justin took no notice at all of what was going on, since he was a man incapable of perception, although he was invariably an eyewitness to all that happened in the Hippodrome. For he was extremely simple, with no more sense than a donkey, ready to follow anyone who pulls its rein, waving its ears all the time. And Justinian both did the things described and threw everything else into confusion too. No sooner had he seized control of his uncle's authority than he eagerly began to squander the tax revenues in the most reckless manner, now that he had become master of them. From time to time he came into contact with some of the Huns and kept showering money on them for services to the state. The inevitable result was that Roman territory was exposed to constant incursions. For after tasting the wealth of the Romans these

barbarians could never again keep away from the road that led to the capital.

Again, he did not hesitate to throw vast sums into erecting buildings along the seafront in the hope of checking the constant surge of the waves. He pushed forward from the shore by heaping up stones in his determination to defeat the onrush of water, and in his efforts to rival, as it were, the strength of the sea by the power of wealth.[35] And he gathered into his own hands the private property of all the Romans in every land, either accusing them of some crime which they had not committed or coaxing them into the belief that they had made him a free gift. Many who had been convicted of murders and other capital crimes made their entire property over to him and so escaped without paying the penalty of their offences. Others, who were perhaps laying claim without any justification to lands belonging to their neighbours and finding it impossible to win judgement in arbitration against their opponents because they had no legal case, would actually make the Emperor a present of the property in dispute and got clear of the whole business; they themselves by generosity that cost them nothing secured an introduction to His Majesty, and by the most unlawful means managed to best their legal adversaries.

Now would not be an inopportune moment, it seems to me, to describe Justinian's personal appearance. In build he was neither tall nor unusually short but of medium height; not at all skinny but rather plump with a round face that was not unattractive, for it retained its healthy complexion even after a two-day fast. To describe his general appearance in a word, he bore a strong resemblance to Domitian, Vespasian's son, whose monstrous behaviour left such a mark upon the Romans that even when they carved up his whole body they did not feel that they had exhausted their indignation against him: the Senate passed a decree that not even the name of this Emperor should appear in writing, nor any statue or portrait of him be preserved. Certainly from the inscriptions everywhere in Rome,

35. See *Buildings* 1.5–9 for a more positive account of Justinian's building work along the Constantinopolitan coastline.

and wherever else his name had been inscribed, it was chiselled out, as can be seen, leaving all the rest intact, and nowhere in the Roman Empire is there a single likeness of him except for a solitary bronze statue, which survived in the following way.

Domitian had a wife, a woman of dignified and decorous birth and general bearing, who had herself never done the least wrong to any man alive or approved of a single one of her husband's actions. Accordingly she was very highly esteemed, and the Senate at this time sent for her and invited her to ask for anything she liked. She made only one request – that she might take Domitian's body and bury it, and set up a bronze statue of him in a place of her own choosing. The Senate agreed to this, and the widow, wishing to leave to later generations a monument to the inhumanity of those who had carved up her husband, devised the following plan. Having collected Domitian's flesh, she put the pieces together carefully and fitted them to each other; then she stitched the whole body together and showed it to the sculptors, asking them to make a bronze statue portraying the tragic end of the dead man. The artists produced the statue with no loss of time, and the widow took it and erected it on the street that leads up to the Capitol, on the right-hand side as you go there from the Forum: it showed the appearance and tragic end of Domitian, and does so to this day. It would seem likely that Justinian's general build, his actual expression and all the characteristic details of his visage are clearly portrayed in this statue.

Such, then, was his outward appearance; his character was beyond my powers of accurate description. For he was both prone to evil-doing and easily led astray – 'both knave and fool' as they say. Nor did he ever speak the truth to those he happened to be with, but in everything that he said or did there was always a dishonest purpose; yet to anyone who wanted to deceive him he was easy prey. He was by nature an extraordinary mixture of folly and wickedness inseparably blended. This perhaps was an instance of what one of the Peripatetic philosophers suggested long ago – that exactly opposite qualities may be combined in Man's nature just as in the blending of colours.

But here I write of matters which I have proven incapable of mastering.[36]

Well, then, this Emperor was dissembling, crafty, hypocritical, secretive by temperament, two-faced; a clever fellow with a marvellous ability to conceal his real opinion, and able to shed tears, not from joy or sorrow but employing them artfully when required in accordance with the immediate need, lying all the time, not carelessly, however, but confirming his undertakings both with his signature and with the most dread oaths, even when dealing with his own subjects. But he promptly disregarded both agreements and solemn oaths, like the most contemptible slaves, who by fear of the tortures hanging over them are driven to confess misdeeds they have denied on oath. A treacherous friend and an inexorable enemy, he was passionately devoted to murder and plunder; quarrelsome and above all an innovator; easily led astray into evil ways but refusing every suggestion that he should follow the right path; quick to devise vile schemes and to carry them out; and with an instinctive aversion to the mere mention of anything good.

How could anyone find words to describe Justinian's character? These vices and many yet greater he clearly possessed to an inhuman degree; it seemed as if nature had removed every tendency to evil from the rest of mankind and deposited it in the soul of this man. In addition to everything else, he was far too ready to listen to false accusations and quick to inflict punishment. For he never made thorough investigation of the facts before passing judgement but on hearing the accusations immediately had his verdict announced. Without hesitation he wrote orders for the seizure of villages, the burning of cities and the enslavement of whole nations, for no reason at all. So that if one chose to add up all the calamities which have befallen the Romans from the beginning and to weigh them against

36. This reeks of false humility, suggesting that Procopius may have regarded himself as something of a philosopher, as A. Kaldellis has argued he was (*Procopius of Caesarea: Tyranny, History, and Philosophy at the End of Antiquity* (Philadelphia: University of Pennsylvania Press, 2004)). Note that I restore the 'not' introduced by Haury and omitted by Williamson.

those for which Justinian was responsible, I feel sure that he would find that a greater slaughter of human beings was brought about by this one man than took place in all the preceding centuries. As for other people's money, he seized it by stealth without the slightest hesitation, for he did not even think it necessary to put forward any excuse or justification before taking possession of a thing to which he had no claim. Yet when he had secured the money he was quite prepared to show his contempt for it by reckless prodigality, or to throw it to barbarians without the slightest need. In short, he kept no money, and allowed no one else in the world to keep any, as if he were not overcome by avarice but held fast by envy of those who had acquired money. Thus he cheerfully banished wealth from Roman soil and became the architect of poverty for all.

[9] The features of Justinian's character, then, as far as I am in a position to state them, were roughly as suggested above. And he married a wife whose origin and upbringing I shall now reveal, as also how, after becoming his consort, she utterly overthrew the Roman state. In Byzantium there was a man called Acacius, a keeper of the circus animals, belonging to the Green faction and called the Master of Bears. This man died of natural causes during the reign of Anastasius, leaving three daughters, Comito, Theodora and Anastasia, of whom the eldest had not yet completed her seventh year. The widow married again, hoping that her new husband would from then on share in the management of her house and the care of the animals. But the Greens' Dancing-master, a man called Asterius, was offered a bribe to remove these two from their office, in which he installed his Paymaster without any difficulty, for the Dancing-masters were allowed to arrange such matters just as they chose. But when the woman saw the whole populace congregated in the circus, she put wreaths on the heads of the little girls and in both their hands, and made them sit down as suppliants. The Greens refused absolutely to admit the supplication, but the Blues gave them a similar office, as their Master of Bears too had died.

When the children were old enough, they were at once put on the stage by their mother, as their appearance was very attractive – not all at the same time, however, but as each one seemed to her to be up to the task. Now the eldest one, Comito, was already famous amongst the harlots of her cohort. Theodora, who came next, clad in a little sleeved number fit for a slave girl, used to assist her in various ways, following her about and invariably carrying on her shoulders the bench on which her sister habitually sat in public. For the time being, Theodora was still too immature physically to be capable of intercourse with a man – that is, to take it as a woman. But she would perform a certain more 'male' lewd favour for those who were hard up, or for slaves, who, when following their owners to the theatre, would seize the opportunity to divert themselves in this revolting manner, and she spent much time in the brothel, engaged in this unnatural physical pursuit. But as soon as she reached puberty and at last was ripe for it, she joined the women on the stage and promptly became a prostitute of the type the ancients called a 'trooper'.[37] For she was not a flautist or harpist; indeed she could not even dance well enough to make it on to the line-up; rather she just sold her youth to passers-by, working with nearly her entire body.

Later she teamed up with the sketch actors at the theatre and took part in their shows there, playing up to their 'get-a-laugh' antics. She was extremely sharp and had a biting wit, and quickly became popular as a result. For there was not an ounce of modesty in the little hussy, and no one ever saw her shocked: she rendered the most shocking services without the slightest hesitation, and she was the sort of girl who, for instance, if somebody beat her up or punched her in the face, would crack a joke about it and roar with laughter; and she would throw off her clothes and exhibit to passers-by both full-frontal nudity and her naked rear – that is, those parts of the female anatomy which the rules of decency require should be kept veiled and hidden from the eyes of men.

She used to tease her lovers by lounging around with them, and by constantly toying with novel methods of intercourse she could always draw the attention of the lascivious to her; so far

37. The Greek refers to the lowest rank of foot-soldier.

from waiting to be approached by anyone she encountered, she herself by cracking dirty jokes and wiggling her hips suggestively would invite all who came her way, especially if they were beardless youths. Never was anyone so completely given up to unlimited self-indulgence. Often she would go to a bring-your-own-food dinner party with ten or more youths, all at the peak of their physical prowess and with sex their trade, and she would lie with all her fellow-diners the whole night through; and when she had worn them all out she would turn to their servants, as many as thirty on occasion, and copulate with every one of them – but even so could not satisfy her lust.

One night she went into the house of a notable during the drinking, and, it is said, before the eyes of all the guests she mounted the protruding part of the couch near their feet and forthwith pulled up her dress in the most disgraceful manner, and did not shy away from displaying her lasciviousness. And though she made full use of three orifices, she often found fault with Nature, complaining that Nature had not made the holes in her nipples larger so that she could devise another variety of intercourse there. Of course, she was frequently pregnant, but by using pretty well all the tricks of the trade she was able to induce an immediate abortion.

Often in the theatre too, in the full view of the people, she would throw off her clothes and stand naked in their midst, having only a pair of knickers over her private parts and her groin – not, however, because she was ashamed to expose these also to the public, but because no one is allowed to appear there absolutely naked: underwear over the groin is compulsory. And with this costume she would spread herself out and lie on her back on the floor. Certain menials on whom this task had been imposed would sprinkle barley grains over her private parts, and geese trained for the purpose used to pick them off with their beaks one by one and swallow them. Theodora, far from blushing when she stood up again, actually seemed to be proud of this performance. For she was not only shameless herself but did more than anyone else to encourage shamelessness. And many times she threw off her clothes and stood in the middle of the actors on the stage, leaning over backwards or pushing out her rear to invite both those who had already enjoyed her and those who had not been intimate as yet, parading her own special brand of gymnastics. With such lasciviousness did she misuse her own body that she appeared to have her privates not like other women in the place intended by nature but in her face![38] And again, those who were intimate with her showed by so doing that they were not having intercourse in accordance with the laws of nature, and a person of any decency who happened to meet her in public would swing round and beat a hasty retreat, for fear he might come into contact with any of the hussy's garments and so appear tainted with this pollution. For to those who saw her, especially in the early hours of the day, she was a bird of ill omen. As for her fellow performers, she habitually and constantly stormed at them like a fury, for she was malicious in the extreme.

Later she accompanied Hecebolus, a Tyrian who had taken over the governorship of Pentapolis,[39] in order to serve him in the most revolting capacity, but she got into bad odour with him and was kicked out without more ado; as a result she found herself without even the necessities of life, which from then on she provided in her customary fashion by making her body the tool of her illegal trade. First she came to Alexandria; then, after making a tour round the whole East, she returned to Byzantium, in every city following an occupation which a man had better not name, I think, if he hopes ever to enjoy the mercy of God. It was as if the unseen powers could not allow any spot on earth to be unacquainted with Theodora's depravity.

Such, then, were the birth and upbringing of this woman, the subject of common talk amongst the women of the streets and among people of every kind. But when she arrived back in Byzantium Justinian conceived an overwhelming passion for her. At first he consorted with her only as his mistress, though he did promote her to Patrician rank. This at once enabled Theodora to obtain vast influence and very considerable wealth.

38. An apparent allusion, now obscure, to a pagan fertility cult in Procopius' native Palestine, where statuettes of a goddess with genitalia in place of her face have been discovered.
39. A group of five cities in Libya.

For, as so often happens to men consumed with passion, it seemed to Justinian's eyes the most delightful thing in the world to lavish all his favours and all his wealth upon the object of his passion. And the whole state became the fuel for this love. With Theodora to help him, he impoverished the people far more than before, not only in the capital but in every part of the Empire. As both had long been supporters of the Blue faction, they gave its members immense powers over affairs of state. It was a very long time before the evil was mitigated to any great extent. It happened in this way.

Justinian suffered from a prolonged illness, which brought him into such extreme danger that he was even reported to be dead. All the time the factionists were misbehaving in the ways already described, and one Hypatius, a man of some distinction, was murdered by them in full daylight in the sanctuary of Sophia. When this crime had been committed, the disorders it provoked were reported to the Emperor, and all those about him, seizing the opportunity provided by Justinian's absence from public affairs, did everything they could to emphasize the gravity of what had occurred, giving him a complete account of all the happenings from beginning to end. At that the Emperor instructed the Prefect of the City to bring all the offenders to justice. This official was named Theodotus but was generally referred to as 'The Pumpkin'. He made a thorough examination of all concerned and was able to arrest many of the perpetrators and sentence them to execution according to the law, although many of them slipped through his fingers and escaped. At a later date they were to rise to prominence in Roman affairs.[40]

Contrary to expectation the Emperor suddenly recovered and actually took steps to get rid of Theodotus as a poisoner and a magician. But as he could invent no possible pretext to justify his destroying him, he subjected some of the man's friends to the most horrible torments and drove them to make accusations against him that were without foundation. Whilst all the others kept out of his way and remained discreetly silent about their distress at Justinian's machinations against Theodotus, Proclus

40. The Greek here is corrupt and cannot be emended with any certainty.

alone, who held the Quaestorship, as it was called, openly
asserted that the accused man was innocent of the charge and
had done nothing to deserve death. In consequence Theodotus,
on the suggestion of the Emperor, conveyed himself away to
Jerusalem. But it came to his knowledge that men had arrived
there who were bent on his destruction; so ever after that he
remained hidden in the sanctuary and never emerged till the
day of his death.

Of Theodotus there is no more to be said. But the factionists
from this time on became the most prudent people in the world.
They no longer ventured to misbehave in such shocking ways,
though they had every opportunity to follow their career of
lawlessness with even greater impunity. Here is evidence
enough: when a few of them later showed similar audacity,
they suffered no penalty whatsoever. For those authorized to
inflict punishment invariably provided the perpetrators of
crimes with every opportunity to evade it, encouraging them
by this connivance to trample on the laws.

As long as the Empress[41] was still alive, it was quite impossible
for Justinian to make Theodora his lawful wife. On this one
point the Empress opposed him, though she objected to none
of his other actions. For the old lady abhorred wickedness,
although she was a peasant and a barbarian by birth, as stated
earlier. She was quite incapable of contributing to government
and remained utterly ignorant of state affairs; in fact she
dropped her real name, which she felt to be ridiculous, before
entering the Palace, and assumed the new name Euphemia. But
some time later it happened that the Empress died. Justin was
in his dotage and quite senile, so that he became the laughing-
stock of his subjects, treated by everyone with complete contempt because of his ignorance of what was happening and left
out of account; Justinian on the other hand was greatly feared
and assiduously courted, for he stirred up trouble all the time,
producing universal turmoil and confusion. This was the
moment he chose for arranging his engagement to Theodora.
But as it was impossible for a man who had reached the rank

41. I.e. Lupicina, wife of Justin.

of senator to make a harlot his wife, such a thing being prohibited from the beginning by the most venerable laws, he forced the Emperor to abrogate the laws by establishing a new one.[42] From that moment he lived with Theodora as his legal spouse, thereby enabling everyone else to get engaged to a harlot. Then as a tyrant he immediately seized upon the imperial office, fabricating an excuse to disguise the high-handedness of his action. He was proclaimed Emperor of the Romans, in conjunction with his uncle, by each of the notables whom overpowering fear compelled to vote in this way. Imperial authority was assumed by Justinian and Theodora three days before the Feast,[43] a time when one is not allowed to greet any of one's friends or to wish him a good day. A few days later, Justin died from natural causes after reigning for nine years,[44] and Justinian alone in conjunction with Theodora took over the empire.

[10] So it came about that Theodora – born, brought up and educated as described – despite all obstacles attained imperial rank. For it never even occurred to her husband that his conduct was shocking, though he was in a position to take his pick of the Roman Empire and select for his bride the most nobly born woman in the world who had enjoyed the most exclusive upbringing, and was thoroughly acquainted with the claims of modesty, and had lived in an atmosphere of chastity, and in addition was superbly beautiful and still a virgin – or, as they say, pert of breast. No: he must needs make the common bane of all mankind his very own, oblivious of all the facts which we have previously disclosed, and consort with a woman double-dyed with every kind of horrible pollution and guilty over and over again of infanticide by wilful abortion.

Not one thing more needs to be mentioned, I think, regarding the character of this man: this marriage would be quite enough to reveal only too clearly all his moral sickness; it was interpreter, witness and chronicler of the course he followed. For when a man cares nothing for the infamy of his actions, and does not hesitate to be known to all and sundry as a

42. Preserved at *Codex Iustinianus* 5.23 (AD 520–23).
43. I.e. Easter.
44. AD 518–27.

revolting character, no path of lawlessness is closed to him, but, armed with the shamelessness visible at every moment in his face, he advances cheerfully and without any misgivings to the most loathsome deeds.

Nor indeed did even one member of the Senate, seeing the state saddling itself with this disgrace, see fit to protest and to oppose such proceedings, though they would all have to fall down before her as if she were a goddess. There was not even one priest who showed any disgust, though they would be obliged to address her as 'Mistress'. And the people who had previously watched her performances in the theatre instantly and disgracefully demanded with upturned hands to be her grovelling slaves in both fact and name. Nor did one soldier resent being called on to face danger on the battlefield for Theodora's benefit; nor did any other living person oppose her. All of them, I imagine, were subdued by the thought that this was the fate assigned to them and accordingly lifted no finger to prevent this revolting state of affairs, as though Fortune had given a demonstration of her power; for as she controls all human affairs it is a matter of complete indifference to her that what is done shall be justifiable, or that men shall feel that there was reason behind what has happened already. Suddenly by an unreasoning display of power she uplifts to a lofty eminence a man who seems to have been entangled hitherto in one difficulty after another; she offers no resistance to anything on earth that he takes in hand, and all things conspire to hurry him along to whatever goal she has seen fit to choose for him, while all mankind stands back without hesitation and makes way for Fortune as she goes ahead.[45] But we must leave it to God to decide how these things shall be and how they shall be spoken of.

As for Theodora, she had an attractive face and a good figure but was short and pallid, though not to an extreme degree, for there was just a trace of colour about her. Her glance was invariably fierce and intensely hard. If I were to attempt a

45. Procopius' musings on Fate bear comparison to those contained in the treatise *On the Consolation of Philosophy* by his Italian contemporary the statesman and scholar Boethius.

detailed account of her life upon the stage, I could go on for
the rest of time, but the few incidents picked out for inclusion
in the preceding account should be enough to give a complete
picture of this woman's character for the enlightenment of
future generations. But now we must sketch the outlines of
what she and her husband did in unison, for neither did anything apart from the other to the end of their joint lives. For a
long time it was universally believed that they were exact oppo-
sites in their ideas and interests, but later it was recognized that
this false impression had been deliberately fostered to make
sure that their subjects did not put their own differences aside
and rebel against them, but were all divided in their feelings
about them. They began by creating a division between the
Christians, and by pretending to take opposite sides in religious
disputes they split the whole body in two, as will shortly be
made clear. Then they kept the factions at loggerheads. The
Empress made out that she was throwing her full weight behind
the Blues, and by extending to them full authority to assail the
opposite faction she made it possible for them to disregard all
restrictions and perform outrageous deeds of criminal violence.
Her husband replied by behaving as if he were boiling over
with bottled-up resentment but was unable to stand up to his
wife overtly, and often they transformed the outward appearance of policy and swopped roles. He, for instance, would insist
on punishing the Blues as criminal offenders, while she in a
faked rage would complain bitterly that, as they say, she had
'yielded to her husband under protest'.

And yet the Blue partisans, as I said before, seemed to be the
most orderly; for they were satisfied that it was quite unjustifiable to go to the limit in doing violence to one's neighbours.
Again, in the bitter animosities aroused by lawsuits, each of the
partners appeared to be backing one of the litigants, and it was
so arranged that victory should go to the one who championed
the unjust cause,[46] and that in this way the two of them should
purloin most of the property of both disputants.

Finally, many were included in this Emperor's list of intimate

46. A reminiscence of Aristophanes' *Clouds*.

friends and raised to positions which enabled them to violate the laws and commit offences against the state to their heart's content, but as soon as it was evident that they had made their pile, they promptly came into collision with Theodora and found themselves in her bad books. At first Justinian was perfectly prepared to declare himself their enthusiastic supporter, but later on his sympathy for the poor fellows would dry up, and his zeal on their behalf would become very uncertain. That would be the signal for his partner to damage them beyond recovery while he, shutting his eyes tight to what was going on, opened his arms to receive their entire possessions, thus shamelessly acquired. In practising these tricks they invariably collaborated, though in public they acted as if they were at variance; thus they succeeded in dividing their subjects, and in so doing strengthened their hold that it could never be shaken off.

[11] Accordingly, when Justinian ascended the throne it took him a very little while to bring everything into confusion. Things hitherto forbidden by law were one by one brought into public life, while established customs were swept away wholesale, as if he had been invested with the mantle of imperial majesty on condition that he would change all things to new forms. Long-established offices were abolished, and new ones set up to run the state's business; the laws of the land and the organization of the army were treated in the same way, not because justice required it or the general interest urged him to it, but merely so that everything might have a new look and might be associated with his name. If there was anything which he was not in a position to transform there and then, even so he would at least attach his own name to it.

Of the forcible seizure of property and the murder of his subjects he could never have enough: when he had looted innumerable households of wealthy people he was constantly on the lookout for others, immediately squandering on one barbarian tribe or another, or on crazy building schemes, all that had been amassed by his earlier looting. And when he had without any excuse got rid of thousands and thousands of people, or so it would seem, he promptly devised schemes for doing the same to others more numerous still.

At that time the Romans were at peace with all mankind, so – not knowing how to satisfy his lust for blood – Justinian kept propelling all the barbarians into collision with one another and, sending for the chieftains of the Huns, though he had no reason at all, with senseless prodigality he flung vast sums into their laps, making out, if you please, that these were pledges of friendship. This he was stated to have done even when Justin was on the throne. They for their part, having received this windfall, used to send some of their brother-chieftains at the head of their men, urging them to make sudden raids into the Emperor's territory, so that they too might be in a position to exact a price for peace from the man who for no reason at all was prepared to pay for it. These chiefs at once began the enslavement of the Roman Empire, and all the time they were in the Emperor's pay. Their example was immediately followed by others who joined in the pillaging of the unfortunate Romans, and on top of that pillage received as a reward for their inroads the extravagant largesse of the Emperor. Thus, in short, from year's end to year's end they all took turns to plunder and pillage everything within their reach. For these barbarians have many groups of chieftains, and the war was passed from one group to another in rotation as a result of Justinian's inexcusable prodigality; it could never come to an end but went on circling around itself month after month, year after year. And so no single patch of ground, mountain, cave or anything else on Roman soil escaped being pillaged at this time, and many places were actually overrun five times or more. These calamities, however, and all those suffered at the hands of Medes, Saracens, Slavs, Antae and the other barbarians have been recounted in my earlier writings; but as I said at the beginning of this present volume, it is essential that I should make clear now where the responsibility lay for all that happened.

To Chosroes Justinian handed over vast sums in gold to secure peace; then with inexcusable disregard of anyone else's opinion he made himself responsible for the breaking of the truce by his determination to effect an alliance with Alemandarus[47] and

47. Al-Mundhir, King of the Empire's Arab clients after Al-Harith.

Why does Justinian enjoy killing?

the Huns who were in alliance with the Persians, a matter which
I believe to have been discussed without concealment in the
account relating to them.[48] While he was stirring up the faction
riots and wars which brought such misery to the Romans, and
fanning the blaze with this one object only, that – by all possible
means – the earth should be filled with human blood and that
still more plunder should fall into his hands, he devised yet
another horrible massacre of his subjects. It happened in
this way.

Throughout the Roman Empire there are many discarded
doctrines of the Christians which they are accustomed to call
'heresies' – those of the Montanists and Sabbatarians and
numerous others which are wont to cause the judgement of
mankind to err. All the adherents of these were ordered to
renounce their former beliefs under threat of many penalties
for disobedience, above all the withdrawal of the right to
bequeath their property to their children or relations. The
shrines of these 'heretics', as they are called, especially those
who professed the doctrines of Arius, possessed unheard-of
riches. Neither the whole Senate nor any other corporate body
within the Roman state could compete in wealth with these
sanctuaries. They possessed treasures of gold and silver, and
ornaments covered with precious stones, beyond description
and beyond counting, and houses and large villages in great
numbers, and a large amount of land in all quarters of the
world, and every other kind of wealth that exists and is named
anywhere on earth, since none of the long line of emperors had
ever interfered with them. A great many others, even though of
orthodox beliefs, depended upon them at all times for their
livelihood, justifying themselves on the grounds that they were
merely following their regular occupations. So by first of all
confiscating the property of these sanctuaries the Emperor
Justinian suddenly robbed them of all they possessed. The result
was that from that moment most of the men were deprived of
their only means of support.

An army of officials was at once sent out in all directions to

48. *Wars* 2.1.12.

Stance on suicide: like Augustine's?

force everyone they met to renounce his ancestral beliefs. In the eyes of the peasantry such a suggestion was blasphemous, so they resolved one and all to stand their ground against the men who made these demands. Many in consequence perished at the hands of the soldiers; many even put an end to their own lives, being foolish enough to think this the most pious course; and the great majority abandoned the land of their birth and went into exile. But the Montanists, who were established in Phrygia, shut themselves up in their own sanctuaries and at once set these buildings on fire, perishing with them for no reason at all. The result was that the whole Roman Empire was one great scene of slaughter and exile.[49]

A similar law being next passed in respect of the Samaritans, tumultuous disorders descended upon Palestine.[50] All who lived in my own Caesarea and the other cities, thinking it foolish to endure any sort of distress for the sake of a senseless creed, discarded their old name and called themselves Christians, managing by this pretence to shake off the danger threatened by the law.[51] Those among them who were at all prudent and reasonable were quite agreeable to remaining loyal to their new faith, but the majority, apparently feeling indignant that in defiance of their wishes they were being compelled by this law to abandon the beliefs they had inherited, very soon defected to the Manicheans and to the Polytheists, as they are called. But all the agricultural labourers at a mass meeting resolved as one man to take up arms against the Emperor, putting forward as the Emperor of their own choice a bandit named Julian, son of Savarus. They joined battle with the soldiers and held out for some time, but in the end they lost the fight and were cut to pieces together with their leader. It is said that a hundred thousand men lost their lives in this engagement, and the most fertile land in the world was left with no one to till it. And for the great landowners, Christians one and all, this affair had

49. For Justinian's persecution of heretics, see *Codex Iustinianus* 1.5.12–22, and *J.Nov.* 3, 37, 42, 43, 45, 109, 131 and 132.
50. Legislation on Samaritans is to be found in *Codex Iustinianus* 1.5.12, 1.5.17, 1.5.18, and *J.Nov.* 45, 103 and 129.
51. See *Codex Iustinianus* 1.5.18.5.

not benefitting anyone besides Justinian

disastrous consequences; for though the land was yielding them no profit at all, they were compelled to pay annual taxes on a crippling scale to the Emperor in perpetuity, since these demands were pressed home relentlessly.

Next he turned the persecution against the 'Hellenes', as they are called,[52] torturing their bodies and looting their property.[53] Many of these decided to assume the name of Christian for appearance's sake in order to avert the immediate threat, but it was not long before they were for the most part caught at their libations and sacrifices and other unholy rites . . . [54] What was done in respect of the Christians I shall explain in an account hereafter.

After that he passed a law forbidding pederasty,[55] not inquiring closely into those acts committed after the passing of the law but seeking out men who had succumbed to this malady some time in the past. The prosecution of these cases was conducted in the most irregular fashion, since the penalty was imposed even where there was no accuser, and the word of a single man or boy, even if he happened to be a slave forced to give evidence most unwillingly against his owner, was accepted as final proof. Men convicted in this way were castrated and paraded through the streets. At first, however, not everyone was treated in this shocking manner, only those who were thought to be either Greens or exceptionally wealthy, or who happened to have offended the rulers in some other way.

Again, they were bitterly hostile to astrologers. Accordingly the official appointed to deal with burglaries made a point of ill-treating them simply because they were astrologers, flogging the backs of many of them and setting them on camels to be shown to jeering crowds all over the city, though they were old men and respectable in every way. Yet he had nothing against them except that they wished to be authorities on the stars in such a place as this. As a result, great numbers of people were constantly slipping away, not only to the barbarians but also

---

52. Adherents of traditional forms of Greco-Roman religion.
53. See *Codex Iustinianus* 1.5.18.4–5.
54. Lacuna in the text.
55. *J.Nov.* 77 and 141, and *Institutes* 4.18.4.

to distant regions under Roman occupation, and so in both countryside and city it was possible to see great masses of strangers. For to avoid being caught, every man was glad to exchange his homeland for another country, as if his own had fallen into enemy hands.

So it was that the possessions of those considered to be prosperous in Byzantium and every other city – that is, after the members of the Senate – were plundered, in the way described, by Justinian and Theodora. How they managed to rob the senators too of all their wealth I will now explain.

[12] There was in Byzantium a man called Zeno, grandson of the Anthemius who had earlier held the imperial office in the West. To serve their own ends they appointed this man Prefect of Egypt and dispatched him there. But Zeno packed all his most valuable effects on board ship and got ready to sail, for he had an immeasurable weight of silver, and vessels of solid gold embellished with pearls and emeralds, and with other stones equally precious. Their majesties then bribed some of those who seemed most trustworthy to remove the precious cargo with all speed and drop firebrands into the hold of the ship, after which they were to inform Zeno that the blaze had broken out spontaneously on the vessel and the entire cargo had been lost. Not long after, as it happened, Zeno died very suddenly, and the two of them promptly took over his estate as his lawful heirs, for they produced a will of sorts, which it was openly rumoured was not of his making.

By similar methods they made themselves the heirs of Tatian, Demosthenes and Hilara, who in rank and all other respects were leading members of the Roman Senate. The property of certain others they acquired by forging not wills but letters.[56] This was how they became the heirs of Dionysius who lived in Lebanon, and of John, the son of Basilius. John had been quite the most distinguished man in all Edessa, but Belisarius had handed him over willy-nilly as a hostage to the Persians, as recounted by me in the previous narrative.[57] Chosroes finally

56. By which Procopius means codicils – see *Digest* 29.7.
57. *Wars* 2.21.27.

refused to let this man go, accusing the Romans of breaking all the agreements under which Belisarius had handed him over; however, he was prepared to sell him as being now a prisoner of war. And the man's grandmother, who was still alive, furnished the ransom, amounting to 2,000 pounds' weight of silver, in the full expectation of redeeming her grandson. But when this ransom had arrived at Dara, the Emperor got to know of it and forbade the completion of the transaction – in order, he said, that Roman wealth might not be transferred to the barbarians. Shortly after this, John fell sick and departed this life; whereupon the chief administrator of the city concocted a letter of sorts which he said John had recently written to him as a friend, to inform him that he desired his whole estate to go to the Emperor. It would be beyond me to list the names of all the others whose heirs they contrived to become.

Until what is known as the 'Nika' insurrection took place,[58] they were content to annex the estates of notables one at a time; but after it took place, as I related in an earlier account, from then on they confiscated at a single stroke the possessions of nearly all the senators. On all moveable property and on the most attractive estate properties they laid their hands just as they fancied, but they set aside those which were liable to oppressive and crushing taxation, and with sham generosity returned them to their previous owners. These people in consequence were throttled by tax collectors and reduced to penury by the ever-mounting interest on their debts, and thus unwillingly dragged out a miserable existence that was no more than a lingering death.

It was for this reason that to me and to most of us these two persons never seemed to be human beings, but rather a pair of blood-thirsty demons of some sort and, as the poets say, 'plaguers of mortal men'.[59] For they plotted together to find the

58. In AD 532 elements within the Constantinopolitan Senate sought to take advantage of a dramatic escalation of factional violence to dismiss Justinian's chief officers, John the Cappadocian and Tribonian, and ultimately to depose the Emperor himself. The revolt was quashed by Belisarius amidst much slaughter. See *Wars* 1.24.

59. Homer, *Iliad* 5.31, and Aeschylus, *Suppliants* 664.

easiest and swiftest means of destroying all races of men and all their works and, assuming human form, became man-demons, and in this way convulsed the whole world. Proof of this could be found in many things but especially in the power manifested in their actions. For demons are discerned as distinct from human beings by a marked difference. In the long course of time there have doubtless been many men who by chance or by nature have inspired the utmost fear, and by their unaided efforts have ruined cities or countries or whatever it might be; but to bring destruction on all mankind and calamities on the whole world has been beyond the power of any but these two, who were, it is true, aided in their endeavours by Fortune, which collaborated in the ruin of mankind, for earthquakes, pestilences and rivers that burst their banks brought widespread destruction at this time, as I shall explain shortly. Thus it was not by human but by some very different power that they wrought such havoc.

It is said that Justinian's own mother told some of her close friends that he was not the son of her husband Sabbatius or any man at all. For when she was about to conceive him she was visited by a demon, who was invisible but who gave her the distinct impression that he was really there with her as a man giving a woman her fill. Then he vanished as in a dream. And some of those who were present with the Emperor late at night, conversing with him (evidently in the Palace) – men of the highest possible character – thought that they saw a strange demonic form in his place. One of them declared that he more than once rose suddenly from the imperial throne and walked round and round the room, for he was not in the habit of remaining seated for long. And Justinian's head would momentarily disappear while the rest of his body seemed to continue making these long circuits. The witness himself, thinking that something had gone seriously wrong with his eyesight, stood for a long time distressed and quite at a loss. But later the head returned to the body, and he thought that what a moment before had been lacking was, contrary to expectation, filling out again. A second man said that he stood by the Emperor's side as he sat and saw his face suddenly transformed to a

So Justinian's a demon?

shapeless lump of flesh: neither eyebrows nor eyes were in their normal position, and it showed no other distinguishing feature at all; gradually, however, he saw the face return to its usual shape. I did not myself witness the events I am describing, but I heard about them from men who insist they saw them at the time.

It is also related that a certain monk highly favoured by God was persuaded by those who lived with him in the desert to set out for Byzantium in order to speak on behalf of their nearest neighbours, who were suffering violence and injustice beyond bearing. On his arrival there he was at once admitted to the Emperor's presence, but when he was on the point of entering the audience chamber and had put one foot across the threshold, he suddenly drew it back and retreated. The eunuch who was escorting him and others who were present urged and encouraged him to go on, but he gave no answer, and as if he had suddenly gone crazy he dashed away back to the apartment where he was lodging. And when his attendants asked him to explain this strange behaviour, we understand that he said straight out that he had seen the Head of the Demons in the Palace, sitting on the throne, and he was not prepared to meet him or ask any favour of him. After all, how could this man be other than a wicked demon, when he never satisfied his natural appetite for drink, food or sleep but took a casual bite of what was set before him and then wandered about the Palace at untimely hours of the night, whilst having a demonic passion for erotic pursuits?

Some of Theodora's lovers, too, say that, while she was still treading the boards, a demon of some sort swooped on them in the night and drove them from the bedroom where they were spending the night with her. And there was a dancing-girl called Macedonia who belonged to the Blues in Antioch and had acquired great influence, for by writing letters to Justinian while Justin was still master of the Empire she could easily destroy any she wished amongst the notables of the East, causing their property to be confiscated for the Treasury. This woman, they say, while welcoming Theodora on her return from Egypt and Libya, saw that she was very annoyed and put out by the insults she had received at the hands of Hecebolius, and by the loss of her money during that trip. So Macedonia decided to console her and cheer her up, reminding her that Fortune was quite capable of playing the benefactress and showering wealth upon her. Then, they say, Theodora declared that actually during the previous night she had had a vivid dream which told her not to worry about money any more: when she reached Byzantium she would go to bed with the Head of the Demons, and would live with him as his wedded wife in every respect, and as a result would become mistress of all the money she could desire.

[13] Such at any rate were the facts as they appeared to most people. The general character of Justinian was such as I have portrayed, but he showed himself approachable and affable to those with whom he came into contact; not a single person found himself denied access to the Emperor, and even those who broke the rules of etiquette by the way they stood or spoke in his presence never incurred his wrath. That, however, did not make him blush when confronting those whom he intended to destroy. In fact he never gave even a hint of anger or irritation to show how he felt towards those who had offended him, but – with a friendly expression on his face and without raising an eyebrow – in a gentle voice he would order tens of thousands of quite innocent people to be put to death, cities to be over-turned and the confiscation of all their money by the Treasury. This characteristic would have made anybody imagine that he had the disposition of a lamb. But if anyone attempted to conciliate him and by humble supplication to beg forgiveness for those who had incurred his displeasure, then, 'baring his teeth and raging like a beast',[60] he would seem to be on the point of exploding, so that none of his supposed intimates could nurse any further hope of persuading him to grant the desired pardon.

He seemed to be a convinced believer in Christ, but this too meant ruin for his subjects; for he allowed the priests to use violence against their neighbours almost with impunity, and when they looted estates next to their own he wished them joy,

60. Quoted from Aristophanes' *Peace* 620.

Is Justinian just stupid?

thinking that in so doing he was honouring the Divinity. When he judged such cases he thought he was showing his piety if anyone for allegedly religious purposes grabbed something that did not belong to him and, after winning his case, went scot-free. For in his view justice consisted in the priests getting the better of their antagonists. And when he himself got possession by unscrupulous methods of the estates of persons living or dead, and gave these as an offering to one of the churches, he would congratulate himself on this cloak of piety – but only to make sure that title to these estates should not revert to their former owners who had been robbed of them.

But he went much further, and to achieve his aims he engineered an incalculable number of murders. His ambition being to force everybody into one form of Christian belief, he wantonly destroyed everyone who would not conform, and that while keeping up a pretence of piety. For he did not regard it as murder so long as those who died did not happen to share his beliefs. Thus he had completely set his heart on the continual slaughter of his fellow-men, and together with his wife he was constantly engaged in fabricating charges in order to satisfy this ambition. The pair of them were almost indistinguishable in their aims, and where there did happen to be some real difference in their characters they were equally wicked, though they displayed exactly opposite traits in destroying their subjects. For in his judgement he was extraordinarily inclined to vacillate, at the mercy of those who at any moment wished to lead him in whatever direction they thought fit – so long as their plans did not involve generosity or loss of profit – and he perpetually exposed himself to gusts of flattery. His fawning courtiers could with the utmost ease convince him that he was soaring aloft and 'walking on air'.[61]

And once as he sat beside him on the Bench, Tribonian said he was quite terrified that sooner or later as a reward for his piety the Emperor would be carried off to heaven and vanish from men's sight. Such laudations, or rather gibes, he interpreted according to his own preconceived notions. Yet if ever

61. An allusion to Socrates in Aristophanes' *Clouds* 225.

by any chance he complimented some person on his virtues, a moment later he would be denouncing him as a scoundrel. On the other hand, when he had poured abuse on one of his subjects, he would veer round and shower compliments on him – or so it appeared – changing about without the slightest provocation. For his thoughts ran counter to his own words and the impression he wished to give.

What his temperament was in regard to friendship and enmity I have already indicated, evidencing for the most part the man's own actions. As an enemy he was determined and undeviating, to his friends most inconstant, so that he actually brought ruin on numbers of people who had been in his favour but never showed friendship to any man he had once hated. Those whom he seemed to know best and to esteem most he soon betrayed, graciously presenting them to his spouse or whoever it might be, to be put to death, though he knew quite well that it was because of their devotion to himself and that alone that they would die. For he could not be trusted in anything except inhumanity and avarice, as all the world could see: to wean him from the latter was beyond the power of any man. For in cases when he refused to listen even to his wife's persuasions, by throwing into the scales the prospect of a big profit to be made from the business she could lead her husband by the nose into any scheme she fancied, however loudly he might protest. For if there were any ill-gotten gain in sight he was always ready to establish laws and to rescind them again.

And his judicial decisions were made not in accordance with the laws he himself had enacted but as he was led by the prospect of a bigger and more splendid promise of monetary advantage. To commit a succession of petty thefts and so deprive his subjects of their property seemed to him to involve him in no discredit at all – that is to say, in cases where he could not grab the lot in one go on some pretext or other, such as by advancing an unexpected accusation or on the pretext of a nonexistent will. And while he ruled the Romans, neither faith nor doctrine about God continued stable, no law had any permanence, no business dealing could be trusted, no contract meant anything. When he dispatched his intimates on some mission, if they happened to do away with a number of those they came up against and to plunder some great sum of money, they immediately seemed to him fit both to be and to be called men of distinction, since they had carried out all their instructions to the letter. But if they treated men with any clemency, when they reported back to him he was ill disposed to them from then on, and indeed actively hostile, and, writing off men of this kind as hopelessly old-fashioned, he called on them for no further service. The consequence was that many made strenuous efforts to convince him of their villainous character, although their regular behaviour was as different as could be. After promising certain people again and again and confirming the promise with an oath or in writing, he immediately contrived to forget it, supposing that such behaviour won him admiration. Justinian regularly behaved in this way, not only to his subjects but also to many of his enemies, as I have stated previously.

He had little need of sleep as a rule, and his appetite for food and drink was unusually small: he did little more than sample a morsel, picked up with his fingertips, before leaving the table. Such things seemed to him an irrelevance, a mere imposition of Nature: time after time he went without food for two days and nights, especially when the days before the festival known as Easter led him in that direction. Then, as I have said, he often went two days without food and chose to live on a little water and a few wild plants, and after sleeping for perhaps one hour he would pass the rest of the night walking round and round. Yet had he been prepared to spend just that amount of time in good works, affairs of state could have enjoyed a very high degree of prosperity. Instead he employed all his natural powers for the ruin of the Romans and succeeded in bringing the whole political edifice crashing to the ground. His prolonged vigils, privations and painful efforts were undergone with this object alone – always and every day to devise bigger calamities for his subjects. For, as observed before, he was extraordinarily keen to invent and swift to execute unholy crimes, so that ultimately even the good qualities in his nature were instrumental in ruining his subjects.

[14] For in the governance of public affairs it was a time of great disorder, and of established customs nothing remained. I will mention a few instances, but all the rest must be passed over in silence, that my account may not go on forever. In the first place, he himself neither possessed any quality likely to enhance the dignity of an Emperor nor attempted to give the impression of possessing it: in speech, dress and mode of thought he was utterly uncouth. Whenever he wished a rescript to be published in his name, he did not send it in the usual way to the holder of the Quaestor's office to be promulgated but thought fit in most cases, in spite of the poorness of his speech, to read it out himself, while a large crowd of bystanders . . .,[62] so that there was no one against whom those wronged thereby could lodge a complaint.

The officials known as *a secretis*[63] were not allowed the privilege of writing the Emperor's secret dispatches – the task for which they had originally been appointed – but he wrote almost everything himself; for instance, whenever it was necessary to commission the public arbitrators, he would lay down the course they must follow in giving judgement. For he would not permit anybody in the Roman Empire to decide any dispute in accordance with his independent judgement but, obstinately going his own way with insane arrogance, himself settled what verdicts were to be given, accepting hearsay evidence from one of the litigants, and without proper investigation promptly cancelled decisions already given, not swayed by any law or principle of justice but undisguisedly succumbing to sordid covetousness. For the Emperor accepted bribes without a blush, since his insatiate greed had robbed him of all sense of shame.

Frequently matters that had been agreed between Senate and Emperor came up for a second and final judgement. For the Senate sat as if in a picture, in a position to control neither its own vote nor its ability to do any good, assembling for the sake of appearance and in fulfilment of an ancient law, since no member of that assembly was permitted even to raise a voice.

62. A verb appears to have got lost here.
63. Confidential clerks.

Rather the Emperor and his consort for the most part made a show of taking sides in the questions at issue, but victory went to the side upon which they had already agreed. If a man had broken the law and felt that victory was not securely his, he had only to fling more gold to this Emperor in order to obtain the passage of a law going clean contrary to all existing statutes. Then if somebody else should appeal to the first law, which had now been repealed, the Emperor was perfectly prepared to re-enact it and substitute it for the new one. There was nothing that remained permanently in force, but the scales of justice wandered at random all over the place, whichever way the greater mass of gold weighing them down succeeded in pulling them. The abode of Justice was now the marketplace, though it had once been the Palace, and there stalls flaunted themselves where not only the administration of justice but even the making of laws too was sold to the highest bidder.

Again, the *Referendarii*,[64] as they are called, were no longer content to convey to the Emperor the petitions of suppliants and merely report to the magistrates as usual what his decision was about the petitioners. Instead they collected the 'unjust reason'[65] from every side and with various impostures and fallacies[66] regularly deceived Justinian, whose temperament laid him open to such cunning ruses. Then as soon as they came out and had barred the litigant from any contact with those with whom they themselves had conferred, they proceeded to extort from these defenceless people as much money as they needed without laying themselves open to retaliation. The soldiers on guard at the Palace used to place themselves alongside the arbitrators in the Imperial Portico and by brute force secure the verdicts they wanted. At the same time all with few exceptions had left their posts and were wandering just as they pleased down ways hitherto barred to them and not to be trodden; things were all rushing along in utter disorder and had ceased to be called by their proper names, and the state resembled one huge gang of

64. Officials who acted as interlocutors between Emperor and petitioners. See *J.Nov.* 10.
65. Borrowed from Aristophanes' *Clouds.*
66. Adapted from Aristophanes' *Knights.*

children playing 'King of the Castle'. I must leave a great deal out, as I indicated at the beginning of this account, but I must make clear who was the first man to persuade the Emperor to accept a bribe whilst sitting in judgement.

There was a certain Leo, a native of Cilicia, madly devoted to money-making. This Leo became a master of flattery, with an uncanny ability for imposing his will on the minds of the ignorant, and he possessed powers of persuasion which assisted him to turn the crass stupidity of the tyrant to the destruction of his fellow-men. This man was the first to persuade Justinian to sell his legal decisions for money. When His Majesty once made up his mind to steal in the manner described, he never looked back; this scandal went on and on and grew bigger and bigger, and anyone who had made it his aim to bring an unjust accusation against some honest citizen went straight to Leo, and by agreeing that a share of the property in dispute should fall to the tyrant and to Leo, he had as good as won his case, in defiance of all justice, before leaving the Palace. This business enabled Leo to pile up riches on an immense scale, and he became the master of much land and did more than anyone else to bring the Roman state to its knees.

Indeed there was no security for those who had entered into contracts, no law, no oath, no written guarantees, no legal penalty, no other safeguard whatsoever except to toss money into the laps of Leo and the Emperor. But not even this could ensure that Leo's opinion would remain constant: he was quite prepared to sell his services to the other side as well. For since he invariably robbed both sides, it never crossed his mind that to treat with supreme indifference those who had put their trust in him and to act against their interests was in any way discreditable. In his eyes, so long as profit came his way, there was no discredit in playing a double game.

[15] So much for Justinian. As for Theodora, her mind was firmly and perpetually fixed upon inhumanity. No one ever persuaded her or forced her to do anything: she herself with stubborn self-will fulfilled her own purposes with all the powers at her disposal, and nobody dared to ask mercy for anyone who incurred her displeasure. Neither the passage of time, nor

surfeit of punishment, nor any kind of appeal, nor any threat of death, though all mankind lives in expectation that it will fall from heaven, could induce her to abate her wrath in the slightest. In short, Theodora was never once known to come to terms with anyone who had aroused her ire, even when he had departed from this life. The dead man's heir inherited the hatred of the Empress like anything else belonging to his father, and bequeathed it to the third generation. For her animosity was ever ready to be aroused to the destruction of other people, and no power on earth could mitigate it.

To her bodily needs she devoted quite unnecessary attention, though never enough to satisfy herself. She was in a great hurry to get into her bath, and very unwilling to get out again. When she had finished her ablutions, she would go down to breakfast, and after a light breakfast she would take a rest. But at lunch and dinner she indulged her taste for every kind of food and drink. Again and again she would sleep for hours on end, by day till nightfall and by night till sunrise. And though she had strayed thus into every path of self-indulgence for so great a part of the day, she thought fit to run the whole of the Roman Empire! If the Emperor entrusted any business to a man without first seeking her approval, such a change of fortune would come upon that man's affairs that very soon after he would be removed from his position with the utmost ignominy and die a most shameful death.

Justinian found it easy to cope with everything, not only because of his tranquil temperament, but because, as remarked before, he had little need of sleep as a rule, and was approachable in the extreme. For there was almost complete freedom for people, even if they were obscure or completely unknown, not only to come into the presence of the tyrant but to converse with him quite freely and be closeted with him in private. But to the Empress's presence even for one of the magistrates there was no admission except at the cost of much time and effort: on every occasion they all had to await her pleasure, waiting like slaves in a small, stuffy anteroom all the time. For it was impossibly risky for any of the magistrates to be absent. Hour after hour they stood on tiptoes, each straining to hold his head higher than those near him in order to catch the eye of the eunuchs emerging from within. At long last and after days of waiting a few of them were called for: they went into her presence trembling with fear and hurried out again as quickly as they could, having merely prostrated themselves and touched the instep of each imperial foot with the edge of their lips. To make any comment or request unbidden by her was completely ruled out. For the state had become a community of slaves with Theodora as slave-driver. To such an extent was the Roman state being brought to nothing, what with the tyrant's temperament, which seemed too easy-going, and Theodora's, which was harsh and implacable. For an easy-going temperament meant instability, whilst an implacable one made action impossible.

If in their attitude of mind and way of life the difference between them was apparent, they were at one in their rapacity, their bloodlust and their utter contempt for the truth. Both of them were the most practised liars, and if anyone who aroused Theodora's ire was alleged to be committing any offence however trivial and insignificant, she promptly fabricated charges which had nothing to do with the accused and blew the matter up to criminal proportions. Endless indictments received a hearing, and a special court was set up to dispose of them.[67] The judges appointed were of Theodora's choosing, and it was their function to contend with each other to see which of them by the inhumanity of his verdict could succeed better than the others in satisfying the Empress's desire. Thus she saw to it that the property of anyone who had offended her should be immediately pocketed by the Treasury, and after having him most cruelly flogged, though he might well be descended from a long line of noble ancestors, she did not hesitate to punish him with either banishment or death. But if by any chance one of her favourites was known to have committed homicide or any other of the major crimes, she mocked and ridiculed the efforts of the prosecutors, and forced them much against their will to shut up about what had occurred.

67. The Greek is unintelligible, and no emendation is convincing.

Moreover, when the fancy took her, she amused herself by turning the most serious matters into a subject for laughter, as if a comedy were being performed on the theatrical stage. For instance, there was one of the Patricians, an old man who had long held public office. I am well aware of his name, but I shall on no account mention it for fear of keeping alive indefinitely the ridicule that befell him. He was unable to collect a large sum owed to him by one of the Empress's servants, and so he went to her in order to accuse the other party to the transaction and to petition her for help in securing his due. But Theodora had advance information and gave instructions to her eunuchs that when the Patrician appeared before her they were to form a circle round him and listen carefully to what she said, indicating what they must say in response. When the Patrician was admitted to the women's quarters, he prostrated himself in the way she always insisted on and, as if on the point of weeping, spoke thus:

Mistress, it is a painful thing for a Patrician to be short of money. For what in other men brings sympathy and compassion is regarded as ridiculous in one of my rank. Anybody else in extreme financial difficulties can inform his creditors of his position and escape immediately from his predicament; but if a Patrician should find himself unable to meet his obligations, he would be terribly ashamed to disclose the situation, and if he did disclose it he would never convince his creditors, who would think it incredible that poverty could be known in such a class of society. If he does convince them, he will inevitably suffer the most shameful and agonizing misery. Well, Mistress, I have both creditors who have lent their money to me and debtors who have borrowed mine. Those who have lent to me are perpetually pressing for payment, and respect for my position in society makes it impossible for me to put them off, while those who are in my debt, not happening to be Patricians, resort to inhuman excuses. I appeal to you therefore, I beg you and implore you to help me secure my due and escape from my present unhappy predicament.

Such was his statement. And the woman replied by intoning, 'Patrician So-and-So', and the chorus of eunuchs chanted their response: 'That's a mighty big hernia you've got there!' When the suppliant renewed his appeal and spoke in very much the same terms as before, the woman repeated her former reply and the chorus their former response, until the poor fellow gave up in despair, prostrated himself in the regulation way, and departing from there returned home.

For most of the year, the Empress spent her time in the suburbs overlooking the sea, chiefly in the place called Herion.[68] This meant a great deal of discomfort for her huge retinue of attendants, for provisions were in short supply, and they were exposed to dangers from the sea, especially if a storm happened to break, or the whale made a sudden attack somewhere in the area.[69] But they[70] were indifferent to the sufferings of all men alive, so long as they themselves could live in luxurious comfort. Theodora's method of dealing with those who had offended her shall be my next subject. Of course I shall mention only a few cases, that I may not seem to be toiling at an interminable task.

[16] When Amalasuntha,[71] in her anxiety to part company with the Goths, made up her mind to change her whole way of life and was thinking of migrating to Byzantium, as has been stated in the previous account,[72] Theodora reflected that the woman was of proud descent and a Queen, besides being extremely attractive in appearance and swift as lightning to find means to her ends, and became suspicious of her splendid and extraordinarily virile bearing, the fickle spirit of her own husband giving her further cause for alarm. She made her jealousy apparent in a far from inconsequential fashion; rather, she

68. On the Asiatic shore of the Bosphorus.
69. Nicknamed Porphyrion, this huge creature was a menace to shipping for half a century.
70. Meaning the imperial pair.
71. Amalasuntha (493–534), daughter of Theoderic the Ostrogoth, succeeded her father in 526 first as regent and then as Queen in Italy, where she found herself locked in a power struggle with her cousin Theodahad that opened the way to Justinian's reconquest of the peninsula.
72. *Wars* 5.2.22.

schemed to ensnare the woman and bring her to her death. Forthwith she induced her husband to send Peter to Italy by himself to act as an ambassador. At his departure the Emperor gave him the instructions detailed in the appropriate section of my work,[73] where through fear of the Empress it was quite impossible for me to tell the true story of what happened. She herself gave him this single command – to remove the woman from this world at the earliest possible moment; and she saw to it that the man was swept off his feet by the hope of ample rewards if he carried out her commands. When he arrived in Italy – for man is incapable by nature of proceeding with hesitation to a brutal murder when he has hopes of some office, perhaps, or a big monetary reward – he approached Theodahad with an offer of some sort and persuaded him to do away with Amalasuntha.[74] As recompense he was awarded the rank of *Magister*[75] and became immensely powerful and hated more than any man alive.

So ended the story of Amalasuntha. In Justinian's employment was a letter-writer named Priscus, utterly villainous and as blustering as any Paphlagonian,[76] just the man to fit in with the character of his master, and only too anxious to please him in the expectation of receiving similar treatment in return. Consequently he very soon accumulated a huge fortune by very shady means. However, on the grounds that he treated her with scorn and put obstacles in her way, Theodora denounced him to her husband. Her first attempts produced no result, but it was not long before she put her enemy on board a ship and dispatched him in mid-winter to a destination of her own choosing. There she had his head shaved and, though he was most unwilling, compelled him to become a priest! The Emperor himself behaved as if he knew nothing at all of what was going on: he made no attempt to discover the whereabouts of Priscus, nor did he ever give him another thought, but sat in silence as

---

73. *Wars* 5.4.17.
74. She was strangled in her bath.
75. *Magister officiorum* – commander of the Palace Guards.
76. An allusion to the punning gibe often applied by Aristophanes to Cleon.

if lost in lethargy whilst not omitting to pocket all that remained of the money that Priscus had left behind.

Suspicion fell upon Theodora of being in love with one of her servants called Areobindus, a lad of barbarian stock but handsome and young, whom she had personally appointed, it so happened, to be her steward. Wishing to refute the charge (though, as they say, she was madly smitten with him), for the moment she made up her mind to maltreat him in the most harsh manner for no reason at all. What happened to him after we have no idea, nor has anyone seen him to this day. For if she chose to conceal anything that was going on, that thing remained unspoken and no reference was ever made to it; anyone who knew the facts was no longer allowed to report them to any of his closest friends, nor might the man who wished to learn of them ask any questions, however curious he might be. For since mankind's first appearance on the earth, no tyrant has ever been regarded with such fear. No one who had given offence stood any chance of escaping detection: an army of spies kept her informed of all that was said or done both in public and in private. In cases where she did not wish the punishment of the offender to be generally known, this is what she used to do. She first sent for the man; then, if he happened to be a person of rank, she would with the strictest secrecy hand him over to one of her attendants with instructions to convey him to the farthest limits of the Roman Empire. At dead of night the attendant would put the offender on board ship shrouded and fettered, and go on board with him. Then at the place appointed by the Empress he would furtively hand him over to someone well qualified for this task, impressing on him that he must keep the prisoner absolutely safe, and forbidding him to say a word to anyone until the Empress felt sorry for the unfortunate creature, or, after dying a lingering death and wasting away for many years as a result of the hardships which he suffered there, he reached the end of his days.

Vassianus, again, one of the Greens, a young man of some distinction, made such uncomplimentary remarks about her that she was furious with him. News of her displeasure soon came to his ears, so he took refuge in the Church of the Archangel.[77] She at once detailed the officer in charge of the people[78] to deal with him, giving instruction that he was not to charge Vassianus for his abuse of her, but rather for sodomy.[79] The officer soon had him out of the sanctuary and tortured him with an unendurable form of punishment. When the people saw a member of the upper classes who had been surrounded with luxury all his life overwhelmed with such agonies, they were immediately cut to the heart, and their groans and laments rose to high heaven as they pleaded for the young man. But Theodora made his punishment even worse: she had him castrated and killed, though he had never been brought to trial, and finished by confiscating his estate for the Treasury. Thus whenever this damned woman worked herself up, no sanctuary was inviolate, no law offered any protection, nor was the intercession of a city's entire population sufficient to save the offender from his doom, nor could anything else on earth overcome her determination.

In the same way Diogenes, because he was a Green, roused Theodora's fury, although he was a charming fellow, very popular with everyone, including the Emperor himself. But that fact did not weaken her determination to charge him slanderously with sexual relations with men. She suborned two of his household slaves and produced them at court to serve both as prosecutors and witnesses against their owner. He was not examined secretly and behind locked doors, as was usual with her, but in open court, with many judges appointed who were men of distinction, in deference to the high standing of Diogenes. The judges, after investigating the case with great thoroughness, came to the conclusion that the evidence of the household servants was not weighty enough to enable them to reach a verdict, especially as they were slave boys. So the Empress locked up Theodore, one of Diogenes' closest friends, in her favourite cells. There she set about her victim with many flattering enticements, and finally with prolonged physical torture.

77. St Michael.
78. The *Quaesitor* – an office established by Justinian; see *J.Nov* 80.
79. That is to say, he was not arraigned for *iniuria* but fell foul of Justinian's crackdown on pederasty. See *J.Nov* 77 and 141.

Since this treatment produced no result, she ordered a strip of leather to be wound round the prisoner's head about his ears and then twisted and tightened. Theodore imagined that his eyes had left their sockets and had jumped out of his head, but he resolutely declined to confess to anything that he had not done. Accordingly the judges ruled that the evidence had failed to substantiate the charge and found Diogenes Not Guilty, and the city with one accord celebrated a holiday in honour of the event.

[17] That was the end of that. But at the beginning of this account I described what Belisarius and Photius and Buzes suffered at her hands. In addition, two members of the Blue faction, of Cilician origin, at the head of a riotous crowd, set upon Callinicus, Governor of the Second Cilicia, and subjected him to physical assault. His groom, who was standing by his side and tried to shield his master, was murdered before the eyes of the governor and the whole populace. The factionalists were convicted of a series of murders culminating in this one, and in accordance with the law the governor sentenced them to death; but when Theodora heard of it, she flaunted her support of the Blues by seizing Callinicus while he was still in office, and without the slightest pretext impaled him over the murderers' grave. And the Emperor, pretending to cry and lament for the murdered man, sat there squealing like a pig,[80] and though he uttered dire threats against those who had perpetrated the outrage he did nothing at all. But the money of the dead man he plundered without the slightest hesitation.

But Theodora also made it her business to devise punishments for sins of the flesh. Prostitutes – more than 500 in all – were rounded up, women who sold their services in public at three coppers a time, just enough to keep body and soul together. They were dispatched to the mainland opposite and were confined in the Convent known as Repentance in an attempt to force them into a better way of life.[81] However, some of them from time to time threw themselves down from the parapet

80. Borrowed from Aristophanes' *Acharnians*.
81. See *Buildings* 1.9.3.

during the night and so escaped being transmogrified against their will.

In Byzantium there were two young sisters. Not only had their father – and his father and grandfather before him – attained the consulship, but their remote ancestors had been some of the most distinguished members of the Senate. These girls had already been married, but the unfortunate deaths of their husbands had left them widowed. Thereupon Theodora picked out two vulgar, revolting creatures with the firm intention of pairing them off with the girls, whom she accused of improper living. Terrified by the prospect, they took refuge in the church of Sophia and, making for the holy baptistery, held on to the font with their hands. But such privations and sufferings did the Empress inflict upon them that in their anxiety to escape from the miseries of their confinement they became reconciled to the lesser evil of the proposed marriages. So it was that for Theodora no place remained unsullied or inviolate. Thus these girls were coerced into matrimony with a pair of beggarly louts far beneath them in station, though there were young aristocrats who would have been delighted to marry them. Their mother, a widow herself, dared not voice her grief or shed a tear over this calamity but steeled herself to attend the betrothal. Later Theodora, anxious to shake off the guilt of her loathsome conduct, resolved to make amends to the young wives at the cost of injury to the public good. She bestowed an office of authority on each of the husbands. But the girls found no consolation even in this, and incurable, intolerable distresses were brought by these men on almost all their subordinates, as I shall show in later accounts. For Theodora had no respect either for office or for the state, nor did anything else matter so long as she accomplished her purpose.

Now it happened that while she was on the stage Theodora had become pregnant by one of her lovers, and, being unusually slow to recognize her unfortunate condition, she tried by all her usual means to procure an abortion; but, try as she might, she could not get rid of the untimely infant, since by now it was not far from acquiring perfect human shape. So, as she was achieving nothing, she was compelled to abandon her efforts and give birth to the child. When the baby's father saw that she was upset and annoyed because now that she was a mother she would no longer be able to employ her body as before, he rightly suspected that she would resort to infanticide, so he took up the child in acknowledgement that it was his and named it John, since it was a boy. Then he went off to Arabia for which he was bound. When he was himself on the point of death and John was in his early teens, the boy learnt from his father's lips the whole story about his mother and, when his father departed this life, performed all the customary rites over him. A little while later he came to Byzantium and made his arrival known to those who at all times had access to his mother. They, never imagining that she would feel any differently from the generality of mankind, reported to the mother that her son John had arrived. Fearing that the story would come to the ears of her husband, Theodora gave instructions that the boy was to come into her presence. When he appeared, she took one look at him and put him in the hands of one of her household whom she regularly entrusted with such commissions. By what means the poor lad was removed from the world of the living I am unable to say, but no one to this day has ever set eyes on him, even since the decease of the Empress.

At that period almost all women had become morally depraved. For they sinned against their husbands with complete impunity, since such behaviour involved them in no danger or harm. Wives proved guilty of adultery were exempt from penalty, as they had only to go straight to the Empress and turn the tables by bringing a countersuit against their husbands – who had not been charged with any offence – and dragging them into court. All that was left to the husbands, against whom nothing had been proved, was to pay twice the amount of the dowry they had received, and as a rule to be scourged and led away to prison – and then once more to watch their faithless partners showing off and inviting the attentions of their paramours more brazenly than before. Many of the paramours actually gained promotion by rendering this service. Small wonder that from then on most husbands, however shocking their wives' behaviour might be, were only too glad to keep their mouths shut and avoid being scourged, conceding every licence to their wives by letting them believe that they had not been found out.

The Empress felt herself entitled to assume control of every branch of public affairs according to her own personal ideas. It was she who filled the offices of Church and State, investigating one point alone and invariably insisting that no honourable or good man should be a candidate for high office – no one in fact who would be incapable of giving effect to her instructions. Again, she arranged all marriages as if by divine right. In her time no contracts of marriage were voluntarily entered into: a man would suddenly discover that he had a wife, not because he had any desire for one, which is the one thing that matters even among the barbarians, but because Theodora willed it. The women thus pushed into marriage found themselves in the same disagreeable situation: they were forced to live with men when they had not the slightest inclination that way. Often the Empress would even fetch the bride out of the bridal chamber at a mere whim, leaving the bridegroom still unmarried and merely declaring in a fit of anger that she disapproved of the match. Among the large number of men she treated this way were Leontius, who occupied the position of *Referendarius*, and Saturninus, son of Hermogenes the *Magister*, both of them just married.

This Saturninus had married a second cousin, a maiden of good birth and excellent character, whose father Cyril had approved the match, Hermogenes having died earlier. No sooner had they shut themselves in the bridal chamber than Theodora seized the groom and carried him off into another one, where in spite of his heartbroken protestations he was married to Chrysomallo's daughter. This Chrysomallo had once been a dancer and later a harlot, but at the time of this incident she was living in the Palace with another Chrysomallo and Indaro. For thence it was that after abandoning the penis and the life of the theatre they managed their affairs. When Saturninus had slept with his new bride and found that she had already been deflowered, he informed one of those close to him that the girl he had married was nothing but damaged goods.

When this comment came to Theodora's ears, she said that he was showing off and had no right to be so puffed up, and ordered her servants to bend him over like any schoolboy. Then she gave his behind a fearsome beating and told him not to talk such nonsense in the future.

What she did to John the Cappadocian has been related in an earlier account.[82] Her actions sprang from her anger against him, which was not due to his offences against the state – she proved this later, when men who treated those under them more outrageously still in no case received such punishment at her hands – but to the temerity he showed in standing up to her in one matter after another, and above all to the damaging accusation which he brought against her to the Emperor, with the result that she and her husband were almost in a state of open war. As I said at the start, I must here at all costs make clear the true reasons for what happened.

When she had locked him up in Egypt after he had undergone all the miseries that I have already revealed, even then she was not satisfied with the punishments she had inflicted on him but kept up a relentless search for false witnesses to bring against him. Four years later she managed to find two Greens belonging to the faction in Cyzicus: they were believed to have taken part in the revolt against the bishop.[83] By means of flattery, arguments and threats she got these two so firmly in her power that one of them, terrified and at the same time elated with the expectations of profit, laid the horrible responsibility for the bishop's murder on the shoulders of John. The other man flatly refused to speak anything but the truth, even though he was stretched on the rack till he seemed certain to die at any moment. And so she was completely baffled in her efforts to get rid of John on this pretext; yet she cut off the right hands of these two young men – of one because he could not be coerced into giving false evidence, of the other for fear her scheming might become clear as daylight. And although this was all going on in public with no attempt at concealment, her

82. *Wars* 1.25.13.
83. Eusebius, Bishop of Cyzicus.

husband pretended that he knew nothing whatsoever about it.

[18] That the Emperor was not a human being but, as stated, a demon in human guise could be demonstrated by considering the magnitude of the calamities which he brought on the human race. For it is by this immensity that the power of the doer is manifested. To make any accurate estimate of the number of lives destroyed by this man would never, it seems to me, be within the power of any living being, or even of God. For sooner could one number all the sands than the hosts of men destroyed by this Emperor. But making a rough estimate of the area which has been denuded of its inhabitants, I suggest ten thousand times ten thousand times ten thousand lost their lives.[84] Libya, for instance, in spite of its enormous size, has been laid so utterly waste that however far one went it would be a difficult and remarkable achievement to find a single person there. Yet the Vandals who took part in the recent armed revolt in that country were 80,000 strong, and the number of their women and children and slaves can hardly be guessed. As for the Libyans who had once lived in the cities and those who worked the land and those who toiled on the sea – as I know only too well since I saw it with my own eyes – how could any man on earth begin to estimate their vast numbers? And even they were few in comparison with the Moorish inhabitants, who perished to a man along with their wives and little ones. Furthermore, many of the Roman soldiers and many of those who had accompanied them from Byzantium lie under the earth. Thus if one insisted that in Libya alone 5,000,000 people lost their lives, he would, I suspect, be understating the facts. The reason was that as soon as the Vandals had been crushed, Justinian took no steps to consolidate his hold over the country and made no plans to ensure that its resources should be secured for him by winning the firm loyalty of the inhabitants. Instead he immediately instructed Belisarius to return home without loss of time, accusing him of political ambitions of which he was entirely

---

84. Procopius' estimate is, of course, no more intended to be taken literally than is St John's *ten thousand times ten thousand and thousands of thousands*, or the *thousands of ten thousands* of Rebekah's progeny in the Bible.

innocent, so that from then on he could order things at his own sweet will and swallow up all the plunder of Libya.

He immediately sent out assessors, if you please, to value the land, and imposed crushing taxation unknown before, and assumed the ownership of all the most valuable estate properties. Then he turned his attention to the Arians, whom he barred from celebrating their customary sacraments.[85] Finally he kept his armed forces waiting for their pay and in other ways made life a burden for his soldiers. The result of all this was an outbreak of revolts that led to widespread destruction. For he could never bring himself to leave well alone: he had an innate passion for throwing everything into confusion and chaos.

Italy, which is at least three times as large as Libya, has been far more completely depopulated than the latter, so proof of the scale of destruction there too will not be far to seek. The responsibility for what happened in Italy has already been made clear earlier.[86] All the blunders that he made in Libya had their counterparts here. And by sending his 'Logothetes', as they are called, to swell the staff on the spot, he instantly overturned and ruined everything.

Before this war began, Gothic rule stretched from Gaul to the boundaries of Dacia, where stands the city of Sirmium. Gaul and Venetia were for the most part under Germanic occupation at the time when the Roman army arrived in Italy. Sirmium and its neighbourhood are in the hands of the Gepids, but all this region, roughly speaking, is completely depopulated. For some died in the war; others succumbed to disease and starvation, which war inevitably brings in its train. Illyricum and the whole of Thrace – that is to say, from the Ionian Gulf to the suburbs of Byzantium, an area that includes Greece and the Chersonnese – were overrun almost every year by Huns, Slavs and Antae, from the day that Justinian took charge of the Roman Empire. In these raids the local inhabitants suffered untold miseries. I believe that in every incursion more than 200,000 of the Romans residing there were killed or enslaved,

85. See *Codex Iustinianus* 1.5.14.
86. *Wars* 8.23.

so that the whole region was turned into a second Scythian desert.[87]

Such were the consequences of the wars in Libya and in Europe. All this time the Saracens were continuously over-running Roman territory in the East from Egypt to the frontiers of Persia, doing their deadly work so thoroughly that the whole of that region was left almost uninhabited: I do not think it possible that any human being, however careful his investigation, will ever find out the numbers of those who perished in these raids. Again, the Persians under Chosroes thrice invaded the rest of Roman territory and razed the cities to the ground. Of the men and women they captured in the cities they stormed and in the various country districts, some they butchered, others they carried away with them, leaving the land completely un-inhabited wherever they happened to swoop. And from the time when they first invaded Colchis, the destruction of the Colchians, the Lazi and the Romans has continued to this day.

However, neither Persians nor Saracens nor the Huns nor the Slav peoples nor any other of the barbarians were lucky enough to withdraw from Roman soil unscathed. During their incursions, and still more during sieges and battles, they came up against many obstacles, and their casualties were as heavy as those of their enemies. For not only Romans but nearly all the barbarians had the benefit of Justinian's bloodthirstiness. As if Chosroes was not bad enough a character himself, Justinian, as I made clear in the appropriate section,[88] provided him with every inducement to go to war. For he took no pains to fit his actions to the circumstance of the moment but did everything at the wrong time. In time of peace or truce he was always treacherously contriving pretexts for aggression against his neighbours; in time of war he slackened off in the most foolish way, showing a woeful lack of energy in preparing for the projected operations, simply because he hated to part with money. Instead of giving his mind to the task in hand, he went in for stargazing and for foolish attempts to determine the

87. An allusion to Aristophanes' *Acharnians*.
88. *Wars* 1.23.1.

nature of God: he would not abandon the war because he was bloodthirsty and murderous by nature, nor could he overcome his enemies because sheer meanness prevented him from tackling essential problems. Thus it is that during his reign the whole earth was drenched with human blood, shed in an unending stream by both the Romans and almost all of the barbarians.

Such, in fine, was the toll of the wars that took place at this time in all parts of the Empire. And when I reckon up the toll of the civil strife that took place in Byzantium and every city besides, my conclusion is that as many lives were lost in this way as in the wars. Justice and impartial punishment for crimes committed were hardly ever seen, and the Emperor gave enthusiastic support to one of the two factions, so naturally their rivals did not lie down either. They all took to desperate courses, utterly heedless of the consequences, the one side because they were the underdogs, the other side because they had the upper hand. Sometimes they went for each other en masse, sometimes they fought in small groups, or again, from time to time they laid traps for individual opponents, and for thirty-two years they never missed one opportunity to practise frightful brutalities against each other, while at the same time they were constantly being sentenced to death by the magistrate responsible for public order. But even so, punishment for the crimes committed fell almost entirely on the Greens. Moreover, the punitive action against Samaritans and so-called heretics filled the Roman Empire with blood. This brief sketch is all that I propose to offer now: I gave a sufficiently detailed account a little earlier.

Such were the disasters which in the time of this demon in human form befell the entire human race, disasters for which Justinian, as the reigning Emperor, provided the causes. The immeasurable distress which some hidden power and demonic nature enabled him to bring upon his fellow-men I shall now go on to reveal. For while this man administered Roman affairs there was a continuous series of catastrophes, which as some maintained were due to the presence here of this wicked demon and to his machinations, though others argued that the Divinity, hating all that Justinian did and turning away from the Roman

Empire, granted the avenging demons licence to effect such things in this manner.

To begin with, the River Scirtus inundated Edessa, bringing on the inhabitants calamities without number, which I shall recount in a later volume.[89] Next the Nile rose in the usual way but failed to subside again at the proper time, bringing upon some of the inhabitants sufferings which I described earlier.[90] Thirdly, the Cydnus poured almost all round Tarsus, inundated the city for days on end and did not subside until it had done incalculable damage there. Again, earthquakes destroyed Antioch, the first city of the East, Seleucia, which is its nearest neighbour, and Anazarbus, the most famous city in Cilicia.[91] The number of lives lost in these three cities it is impossible to estimate; and we must not forget Ibora and Amasia, the first city in Pontus, or Polybotus in Phrygia, and the city which the Pisidians call Philomede, or Lychnidus in Epirus, and Corinth, all of which had huge populations for centuries past. Every one of these cities has been overthrown by an earthquake during this short period, and the inhabitants almost without exception have perished with them. On top of the earthquakes came the plague which I mentioned before;[92] this carried off almost half the survivors. On such a vast scale was the loss of life, first while this man was administering the Roman state and later when he held the imperial title.

89. A promise fulfilled in *Buildings* 2.7.2. The flood took place in 525.
90. *Wars* 7.29.6.
91. Major quakes occurred in 526 and 542.
92. *Wars* 2.22–3.

PART III
ANATOMY OF A REGIME

[19] I shall now proceed to relate how he appropriated all the money he could lay his hands on, first mentioning a dream-vision which at the beginning of Justin's reign appeared to one of the notables. He reported how in his dream he seemed to be standing somewhere in Byzantium on the seashore exactly opposite Chalcedon, and that he saw Justinian standing in front of him right in the middle of the channel. First Justinian drank up all the water of the sea, so that from then on he seemed to the dreamer to be standing on dry land, as the waves did not break on the shore at this point; then more water appeared there, choked with masses of filth and rubbish and pouring out of the sewers on both sides. This Justinian drank up as well, laying bare once more the bed of the channel.

This was what the man saw in his dream-vision. When his uncle Justin ascended the throne, Justinian found the state full to the brim with tax revenues. For Anastasius had shown himself the most stewardly and bursarial of all the Emperors, and, fearing – with good cause – that his successor might find himself short of money and be tempted to plunder his subjects, he had filled to overflowing with gold all the treasuries before he reached the end of his days. All this Justinian dissipated in next to no time, partly on constructions on the shore which served no useful purpose, partly on friendship with the barbarians. Yet one would have expected this sum to keep even a most profligate Emperor amply provided for a hundred years. For it was emphatically stated by those in charge of the coffers of revenue and expenditure[93] and all the other aspects of the public finances that Anastasius, after reigning over the Romans for more than twenty-seven years, had left thirty-two hundred *centenaria* of gold in the public purse. But they say that in the nine short years of Justin's reign this man Justinian created such confusion and disorder in the body politic that no less than four thousand *centenaria* were brought into the state by illegal means; yet nothing whatever was left of all that accumulated wealth – while Justin was still alive, this fellow squandered the lot in the manner already described. As for the sums which in his lifetime he managed to appropriate to himself illicitly and then expend, there are no means of account or reckoning or measure. Like an overflowing river he daily ravaged and despoiled his subjects, but the whole flood swept straight on to enrich the barbarians.

As soon as he had thus dispensed with the public wealth, he turned his eyes towards his individual subjects and lost no time in stripping most of them of their estates, which he seized by brute and unjustified force, hauling up before him on trumped-up charges those who were thought to be well off in Byzantium and in every city besides. Some he accused of polytheism, some of professing doctrines held to be unorthodox amongst the Christians, some of pederasty, others of sexual relations with nuns or other improper forms of intercourse, others of provoking uprisings, or of attachment to the Green faction, or of treachery, or of any other named crime whatsoever, arbitrarily making himself the heir of deceased persons, or even of the living if he saw a chance, claiming that he had been adopted by them.[94] These were his most distinguished

93. Tax collection was overseen by the office of the Praetorian Prefect, whilst imperial expenditure was administered by the Count of the Sacred Largesses and his staff.

94. For legislation on heretics, see *Codex Iustinianus* 1.5.12–22, and *J.Nov.* 3, 37, 42, 43, 45, 109, 131 and 132; for polytheism, see *Codex Iustinianus* 1.5.18.4–5; for sexual crimes, see *Codex Iustinianus* 1.5.12–22, and *J.Nov.* 77 and 141; for nuns, see *Codex Iustinianus* 1.3.53 and 9.13.1, and *J.Nov.* 123 and 37.

deeds. The way in which he turned to his own advantage the insurrection against him known as 'Nika', and immediately became heir of every senator, I explained a little way back,[95] also the way in which before the insurrection he had appropriated to himself, one at a time, the estates of a considerable number of them.

And he lost no opportunity to lavish vast sums of money on all the barbarians – on those to east, west, north and south, as far as the inhabitants of Britain and, indeed, all the tribes there be in every part of the inhabited world, even those of which not even a rumour had ever before reached our ears, and whose names we learnt only when we at last saw them with our eyes. For when they heard what sort of man he was, they did not wait for an invitation: from every direction they poured into Byzantium to get in touch with him. And he was not in the least dismayed but delighted at the whole business, deeming it an unexpected piece of luck to be able to ladle out Roman wealth and toss it to the barbarians or indeed the waves of the sea; and day after day he continued to send them home, every one of them with masses of money. Thus it is that all the barbarians have become in every respect the masters of the wealth of the Romans, either by receiving the money from the Emperor's hand, or by plundering the Roman realm, or by selling back their prisoners of war, or by demanding money in return for a truce. In this way the dream-vision which I related a little way back was fulfilled for the man who saw it. There were yet other methods which Justinian managed to devise for despoiling his subjects, and which without more ado I shall describe to the best of my ability – methods which made it perfectly simple for him to plunder the estates of all of his subjects, not all at once but bit by bit.

[20] First, he made it his practice to set up in authority over the people in Byzantium a prefect who, whilst sharing the annual profits with those who owned the market stalls, was minded to give them permission to sell their merchandise at

95. See chap. 12.

whatever price they liked.[96] And the impact of this on the consumers was that they had to pay three times the price for their provisions, and there was no one to whom they could complain about it. A great deal of harm resulted from this business. For since the state received a share of these profits, the official responsible for these matters was only too happy to enrich himself from this source. Next the subordinates to whom the official had delegated these unsavoury duties, joining forces with those who owned the shops, grasped with both hands this freedom to break the law, and treated abominably those who had no choice but to buy there and then, not only collecting, as has been said, monstrously inflated prices but practising unspeakable frauds in the quality of the commodities sold.

His second step was to establish many 'monopolies', as they are called, selling the welfare of his subjects to those who were prepared to operate this monstrosity. He himself went off with the payment which he had exacted as his share of the bargain, while those who had come to this arrangement with him were allowed to run their business just as they pleased. He behaved in the same unscrupulous way without any attempt at concealment in dealing with all the other magistracies. For since the Emperor always pocketed his own little share of their ill-gotten gains, so too did the magistrates and those immediately responsible for each deal plunge all the more recklessly into the plundering of all who fell within their embrace.

As if the ancient magistracies were not adequate for this purpose of his, he invented two additional ones for the management of public business, though hitherto all indictments had been dealt with by the magistrate set in authority over the people.[97] But to ensure that the number of professional informers should be constantly increasing, and to facilitate yet further the subjection of perfectly inoffensive persons to physical ill-usage,

96. The prefect referred to is the Urban Prefect of Constantinople, whom Justinian ordered to reimpose price controls in the wake of the advent of the bubonic plague: see *J.Nov.* 122 (co-addressed to the Praetorian Prefect of the East, and thus of Empire-wide effect).

97. That is, the populace of Constantinople, i.e. the Urban Prefect.

he made up his mind to create these two new offices.[98] The holder of the one was appointed supposedly to bring thieves to justice, receiving the title of Praetor of the Plebeians; the holder of the other was charged with the correction of habitual pederasts and of those who had illegal intercourse with women, and, as ever, those who did not show orthodox reverence for the Divinity. This official received the title of *Quaesitor*. Now then, the Praetor, if among the stolen goods he put his hands on any articles of great value, made it his business to hand these to the Emperor, explaining that it was impossible to discover their owners. In this way the Emperor always contrived to secure a share of the most valuable plunder. The one called *Quaesitor*, when he had finished with alleged offenders, would hand over to the Emperor as much as he thought fit, without seriously impairing his own capacity to enrich himself illegally at the expense of other people. For the subordinates of these magistrates never produced any accusers, and never called anyone to give evidence of the alleged offences, but through all this time the long line of those unlucky enough to fall into their clutches, though neither accused nor proved guilty, were with the utmost secrecy murdered and stripped of their property.

Later this bloodthirsty murderer instructed these officials and the magistrate responsible for the populace to deal indiscriminately with all accusations, telling them to compete with each other to find out which of them could destroy the greatest number in the shortest time. It is said that one of them promptly asked him, if one day someone were to be denounced by all three of them, which one should have jurisdiction in the case. The answer came at once – whichever of them got his nose in first.

Again, he meddled most improperly with the office of the magistrate called the Quaestor, an office which had been treated, almost without exception, with the greatest respect by previous Emperors, who saw to it that the highest standard of general experience, and above all of skill in legal matters, should

98. The 'Praetor of the People' and the *Quaesitor*; see *J.Nov.* 11, 13, 14, 16, 18 and 80.

be required in holders of this office, who must in addition be manifestly incapable of accepting a bribe; for the consequences would be calamitous for the state if holders of this office were either hampered by any want of experience or given over to avarice. This Emperor on the other hand began by appointing to this office Tribonian, whose activities were described in detail in earlier accounts.[99] When Tribonian departed this life, Justinian purloined a portion of his estate, although he had left a son and a number of grandchildren when he was overtaken by his last day on earth. Junilus, a Libyan by race, was chosen to fill the vacancy, though he had not even a nodding acquaintance with the law, since he was not a practising member of the Bar. He had a good knowledge of Latin, but as regards Greek he had never even been to grammar school and could not get his tongue round the language – why, often when he did his best to pronounce a Greek word, he moved his subordinates to scornful laughter. He had an overwhelming passion for making money in dirty ways: he actually put documents signed by the Emperor up to public auction without the least shame, and in return for a single gold coin he unblushingly held out his palm to all and sundry. For a period of seven whole years these goings-on made the state an object for ridicule. When Junilus too came to the end of his days, the Emperor gave this office to Constantine, who had some training in the law but was absurdly young and had no experience hitherto of lawyers' wrangles – and he was the biggest thief and the biggest boaster alive.

This man had wormed his way deep into Justinian's affections and had become one of his dearest friends; at no time did the Emperor hesitate to use him as a tool either in stealing or in manipulating the law-courts. So it was not long before Constantine made a great pile of money and became unbearably pompous, 'walking on air and contemplating the entire human race with scorn'.[100] If people were prepared to hand over a great deal of money to him, they had to deposit it with some of his most

99. *Wars* 1.24.16.
100. A second reminiscence of the description of Socrates in the *Clouds*.

trusted assistants; then they were free to put into effect the plans they had in mind. But to meet the Quaestor himself or to have any contact with him was impossible for anyone at all, unless he caught him running to the Palace or returning from there – never at a walk but in great haste and at great speed, to make sure that those who came near him did not waste his time without paying for it.

[21] Such were the methods of Justinian in this sphere of operations. As for the Praetorian Prefect, every year he levied more than thirty *centenaria* of gold on top of the public taxes. To this impost he gave the name 'air tax' – to show, I suppose, that this was not a regular or permanent tax, but that by some lucky chance it always seemed to drop out of thin air into his lap. These practices might better be described as an exhibition of his villainy. In the name of this tax, holders of this office grew continually bolder in their plundering of the common people. The proceeds were supposed to be handed over to the Emperor, but the officers acquired a princely fortune for themselves without the slightest trouble. Justinian, however, saw no need to take the least notice of such things;[101] he looked forward to the day when they had a really big pile, for then he could at once bring against them some charge or other to which there was no answer, and there would be nothing to prevent him from depriving them at a stroke of everything they possessed. This was the treatment that he meted out to John the Cappadocian.

Everyone, of course, who occupied this position during the period in question suddenly found himself rich beyond his dreams. There were just two exceptions. One was Phocas, whom I described in an earlier account as a man of unshakeable integrity:[102] he resisted all temptation to enrich himself while in office. The other was Bassus, who did not assume the office till a later date. But neither of these two retained the position for a single year; on the grounds that they were useless and quite out of touch with the age they lived in, they were ousted from

---

101. In fact peculation on the part of tax collectors was a constant complaint of Justinian's; see, for example, the preface to *J.Edict* 13.
102. *Wars* 1.19.18.

their position within a few months. But I must not go into minute detail and drag my story out interminably: I need only say that the same things were going on in all the other government departments in Byzantium.

Everywhere in the Roman Empire Justinian followed this method. Picking out the most cunning of men, he would sell them in return for great sums of money the governmental responsibilities that were to be corrupted by them.[103] For no man of any decency or any vestige of good sense would ever think of pouring out his own money for the pleasure of robbing the innocent. Then, after collecting the cash from those with whom he was negotiating, he gave them permission to do anything they liked to their subjects. This enabled them to ruin all the districts allotted to them, inhabitants and all, and make enough money to keep themselves in luxury for the rest of their lives. To find the money to pay for their cities, they obtained a loan from the bank at a very high rate of interest and handed the money over to the vendor; then when they arrived in the cities, they brought every variety of misery upon their subjects, having no other object in life than to make sure that they could satisfy their creditors and themselves be ranked amongst the super-rich. The business did not lay them open to any risk or criticism; on the contrary, it brought them a good deal of admiration, which became greater and greater as they succeeded in the senseless killing and despoiling of more and more of their chance victims. For to call them murderers and despoilers was to give them credit for vigour and effectiveness. But the moment Justinian noticed that any of these officeholders had amassed a fortune, he netted them on some charge or other and straightaway snatched from them all their money.

Later he made a law that candidates for offices must swear that they would faithfully keep their own hands clean from all thieving, and would neither give nor receive any payment in connection with their official duties.[104] And he laid all the curses

103. The passage here is corrupt, but Procopius may be referring to the appointment of fiscal officers termed *vindices* whose responsibilities, it would appear, were put out to tender to great landowners.

104. See *J.Nov.* 17 and 8.

that have come down from the distant past on anyone who
deviated from his written instructions.[105] But the law had been
in force less than a year when he himself, scorning the written
instructions and oaths and the disgrace involved, began with
less hesitation than ever to bargain over the prices of the various
offices, not in some dark corner but in blatant public. Naturally
those who bought the offices, regardless of their oath, looted
everything still more recklessly than before.

Later still he contrived yet another, quite breathtaking
scheme. Those governorships which he considered the most
important in Byzantium and the other cities he decided that he
would not continue to sell as before. Instead he sought out
hirelings to fill the vacancies, arranging with them that in return
for a salary of some sort they should hand all the loot over to
him.[106] They, on receiving their salaries, blithely set to work
collecting and carrying off everything from the whole countryside, and a hireling authority went out in all directions plundering the subjects in the name of the governorship. In this way
the Emperor, calculating with the greatest care, all the time put
in charge of affairs those who without any doubt were the
biggest scoundrels in the world, and he always managed to
track down this loathsome quarry. In fact, when he installed
the first batch of scoundrels in office and the licence which
power gave them brought their evil dispositions to light, we
were utterly astounded that human nature could accommodate
such immense wickedness. But when in the course of time their
places were taken by others who were able to go far beyond
them, people began to ask each other how it came about that
those who a little while ago seemed the most utter scoundrels
were so amazingly outdone by their successors that they now
appeared to have behaved like perfect gentlemen in all their
proceedings. The third batch in turn outdid the second in every
kind of iniquity, only to be followed by others who by their
ingenuity in dragging people into court surrounded the memory

105. Again, *J.Nov.* 17.
106. See the schedule of governors' stipends appended to *J.Nov.* 8 and the
     details concerning the stipend of the Augustal Prefect of Alexandria in
     J.Edict 13.

of their predecessors with an odour of virtue. As things went from bad to worse, all men came to learn by experience that man's innate wickedness knows no limit: when it feeds on the knowledge of those who have come before, and when the licence which impunity bestows encourages it to victimize all whom it encounters, it seems to swell inevitably to such proportions that it is not even possible for the minds of the sufferers to grasp its immensity.

Such were the miseries the Romans underwent at the hands of those who governed them. Over and over again when an army of enemy Huns had plundered the Roman Empire and enslaved the inhabitants, the Thracian and Illyrian commanders planned to attack them as they retired, but they reversed their decisions when they were shown a letter from the Emperor Justinian forbidding them to launch their attack on the invaders, since they were needed as allies of the Romans against the Goths, perhaps, or against some other of their enemies. The result was that these barbarians began to act as open enemies and to plunder and enslave any Romans within reach; then with their prisoners and other booty they would, in their capacity as friends and allies of the Romans, return to their own homes. Over and over again some of the agricultural workers of those parts, impelled by longing for their wives and children who had been carried off as slaves, made a united assault on the retreating enemy and succeeded in killing numbers of them and capturing their horses together with all the booty – only to find that the consequences of their action were very painful indeed. For a body of men dispatched from Byzantium took it upon themselves without the slightest hesitation to assault them and beat them in addition to imposing fines, until they handed over all the horses they had taken from the raiders.

[22] When the Emperor and Theodora had got rid of John the Cappadocian, they wanted to appoint a successor; so they made concerted and strenuous efforts to find someone still more degraded, looking round for such an instrument of their tyranny, and minutely investigating the temperaments of the candidates, in the hope of ruining their subjects even faster than before. For the time being they chose Theodotus to fill John's

place, not a good man by any means, but not bad enough to fit the bill completely. After doing so they continued their painstaking scrutiny in all directions. To their surprise they found a money-changer of Syrian origin called Peter and surnamed Barsymes. For years he had stood behind the counter changing bronze coins and making an inexcusably high profit out of the transaction, having a very clever knack of filching the copper coins and deceiving one customer after another by the quickness of his fingers.[107] He showed remarkable dexterity in pocketing the property of any who came his way, and if caught he instantly swore his innocence and covered up the misdemeanour of his hands with the effrontery of his tongue. And when he had been enrolled on the staff of the Praetorian Prefecture, he pursued so lawless a course as to delight Theodora and helped her enthusiastically to overcome the difficulties in her own unscrupulous plans. So Theodotus, whom they appointed to succeed the Cappadocian, was immediately relieved of his office and replaced by Peter, who performed their wishes in every particular. He robbed the soldiers on active service of their pay and allowances without ever giving a hint of shame or fear. He even put up governmental functions for auction more brazenly than ever before, and, lowering their prestige, he used to sell them to those who did not shrink from engaging in this unholy traffic, expressly authorizing purchasers of the offices to treat the lives and property of their subjects in any way they chose. For it was agreed at once between Peter and the man who had put down the price for the tax district that he should have licence to plunder and pillage as he liked.[108] Thus there proceeded

107. The sixth-century monetary system was essentially bimetallic. The gold coin, or *solidus*, was the standard unit of account of the Roman state and the imperial aristocracy, and accordingly taxes and rents were reckoned in it. The copper coin, or *follis*, was that most commonly used by more humble members of society, and accordingly the rate of exchange between gold and copper played a major role in intensifying or abating social tensions.

108. Here, with Williamson, I read *choras* (relating to a region or country district: the territory within the fiscal unit administered from a city) rather than Haury's *archês* (for a governmental function or office). Again, what appears to be referred to is the tendering of responsibilities for tax collection rather than the sale of offices per se.

from the very apex of the Roman state a wholesale trade in human lives, and with him the bargain was struck for the destruction of the cities.[109] Through the chief law-courts and round the open forum strode a licensed bandit who defined his duties as the collection of the sums handed over in payment for governmental responsibility. There was of course no hope that there would be a reversal of these misdemeanours. Then again, of all those employed as subordinates in this department of state – they were both numerous and distinguished – he invariably attracted to himself the most cunning and wicked. Such misconduct, alas, was not practised by him alone but rather by all the earlier and later occupants of this office.

Similar abuses occurred in the department of the *Magister*, as he is called, and amongst the Palatine officials whose duties are to attend to financial matters: with the *privata*, as they are called, and the *patrimonium* – in fact, in all the positions of responsibility established in Byzantium and the other cities.[110] For from the time that this tyrant took charge of affairs, in every office the revenues belonging to those administering the business on the ground were commandeered without any justification, sometimes by Justinian himself, sometimes by the head of the department, and those who served under them were reduced to extreme penury and had to work all the time as if they were the lowest of slaves.[111]

A very large quantity of grain had been conveyed to

---

109. Conservative authors such as Procopius and his contemporary John Lydus felt that such arrangements undermined the fiscal cohesion of the city councils that were a characteristic feature of Greco-Roman civilization.

110. Whereas the income and expenditure administered by the Praetorian Prefect and the Count of the Sacred Largesses derived from tax revenues, the departments of the *res privata* ('private property') and *sanctum patrimonium* ('sacred' or 'imperial patrimony') handled the proceeds of state-owned property, a portion of which was held to be at the personal disposal of the Emperor.

111. In *J.Edict* 13 we are informed what proportion of the tax revenues collected in Egypt could be spent on local purposes by imperial officials and civic officers, and what proportion was to be passed on to Constantinople. If local administrators sought to hold on to any more than Justinian or John the Cappadocian had permitted, dire consequences would ensue.

Byzantium,[112] but after most of it had rotted away, he himself compulsorily assigned it proportionately to all the cities in the east, though it was unfit for human consumption, and he compulsorily assigned it not at the rate at which top-quality grain is usually sold but at a much more expensive price.[113] After pouring out vast sums of money to meet these inflated prices, there was nothing that the purchasers could do except to dump the grain in the sea or in a sewer. There was still a large store of sound grain that had not yet gone rotten; this too he decided to sell to the very great number of cities that were short of grain. By this means he made double the money that the Treasury had previously credited to the tax-payers in return for the grain.[114] The next year, however, the harvest of the fields was not nearly so abundant, and the grain fleet arrived at Byzantium with quite inadequate supplies. So Peter, not knowing how to deal with this situation, thought it best to purchase a great quantity of grain from the estate properties in Bithynia, Phrygia and Thrace. And those who dwelled there were obliged to undertake the heavy task of carrying the cargoes down to the coast and to convey them at their own liability to Byzantium, where they received from him trifling payments in return. And their loss amounted to such a huge total that they would have been glad if they had been allowed to present their grain to the state by way of gift and to hand over an additional sum for the privilege. This is the burden that they commonly call the 'requisition'.[115] But even so there was still insufficient grain in Byzantium to meet the demand, and many people protested vigorously to the Emperor about the state of affairs. At the same time almost all the military, as they had not received the pay to which they

112. Constantinople was dependent for its food supply on the shipment of grain from Egypt: see *J.Edict* 13.

113. Other cities in the vicinity of Constantinople were obliged to buy up such grain as was surplus to the capital's needs in what was known as the *epibolê*, or compulsory assignment.

114. Grain collected by way of tax payments in Egypt was reckoned at a nominal cash sum; Peter Barsymes, Procopius claims, sold the grain at double that amount.

115. In Greek *synônê*: compulsory purchase by the state of goods required at a price determined by the imperial authorities.

were entitled, gave themselves up to disorder and constant disturbances all over the city.

The Emperor now made it clear that he was dissatisfied with Peter: he wished to remove him from office, both for the reasons mentioned and because he had been informed that Peter had salted away a fantastic amount of public money which he had managed to embezzle. And such was indeed the case. But Theodora refused to let her husband do this; for she was extraordinarily attached to Barsymes, apparently on account of his sheer wickedness and his more than brutal treatment of those under him. She herself, of course, was utterly ruthless and full to bursting with inhumanity, and she expected her subordinates to be as like herself as possible in character. But they say that she was bewitched by Peter and compelled against her will to show him favour; for sorcerers and demons were an obsession with this man Barsymes, and he was lost in admiration of the Manichees, as they are called, whom he never hesitated to champion publicly.[116] Yet even when she heard about this the Empress did not withdraw her favour from her protégé but made up her mind to give him still more protection and show him still more affection on this account. For from her very childhood she had herself consorted with magicians and sorcerers, as her whole way of life led her in that direction, and to the very end she put her trust in these arts and made them at all times the ground of her confidence.

It is said too that it was not so much by cajolery that she got Justinian under her thumb as by the compelling power of demons. For Justinian was not a gracious or just person, or so unshakably virtuous as ever to be proof against such subtle attacks; on the contrary he was unmistakably the slave of his passion for bloodshed and money-making, and powerless to resist deception and flattery. Even in matters which roused him to the greatest enthusiasm he would do an about-turn for no reason at all, and he had become as unsteadfast as a cloud of

116. Followers of the third-century Persian prophet Mani who expounded a rigorously dualist cosmology. Although persecuted by Sasanian Shahs and Roman Emperors both pagan and Christian, Manichaeism exercised considerable influence on spiritual life in the late antique Near East.

dust. Consequently not one of his relations, or even of his acquaintances, ever placed any real confidence in him: he was forever changing his mind about what he proposed to do. Thus, being as we have said an easy target for sorcerers, he quickly submitted to Theodora as well: nothing did more than this to increase the affection of the Empress for Peter as a devotee of these arts. So it was no easy task for the Emperor to remove him from the office he had occupied hitherto, and, not long afterwards, Theodora insisted on his appointing him Governor of the Treasuries, taking this office away from John, who had been installed in it only a few months before.[117]

John was a Palestinian by birth, a man of very gentle and kindly disposition, who never dreamed of finding means to enrich himself and had never done any harm to any man alive. Not surprisingly he was regarded with extraordinary affection by the whole populace. That was enough to make him thoroughly distasteful to Justinian and his precious spouse; for the moment they unexpectedly found a true gentleman among their ministers, they lost their heads and were so upset that they made furious efforts to dislodge him at the first opportunity by any and every device. So it was that this man John was displaced by Peter, who took charge of the imperial finances and once more became the man chiefly responsible for great disasters involving everyone. He cut off the bulk of the money which by long-established custom was doled out to many every year by the Emperor by way of 'consolation', while he himself unscrupulously piled up wealth at the public expense, handing a small percentage of it to the Emperor. Those who had been robbed of their money sat around in great dejection, especially as he took it upon himself to make the gold coinage smaller, something that had never happened before.[118]

Such were the Emperor's dealings with respect to those who governed. I will now go on to explain how Justinian everywhere

117. Peter's appointment was actually to the office of Count of the Sacred Largesses, for which Procopius is attempting to find a circumlocution.
118. A reference to the series of 'light-weight' gold coins which were issued under Justinian, most probably in response to a shortfall in income resulting from the demographic impact of the bubonic plague.

ruined the great landowners.[119] When a little while ago we mentioned the officials dispatched to all the cities, there was no need for us to do more than outline the sufferings of the general population. For the lords of the villages were the first to be attacked and plundered by these officials;[120] even so, the rest of the story shall be told in full.

[23] In the first place, it had been the custom for centuries past for every ruler of the Roman Empire, not once but repeatedly, to remit to all his subjects their tax arrears, and that with two objects in view – to make sure that those whose capital was exhausted and who had no means of clearing their debts were not subjected to continual pressure, and to avoid furnishing the tax-collectors with excuses for attempting to inform against men who were liable to the tax but owed nothing; but the present Emperor has let thirty-two years go by without doing anything of this kind for his subjects.[121] This meant that those who had no money left had no option but to flee the country and never return. And the informers kept persecuting the more well-to-do landowners[122] by threatening to prosecute them on the grounds that for years they had been paying their dues at a lower rate than the payment required of estate property. For not only did these unfortunate people shudder at the new level of taxation: they were appalled at the thought of being crushed beneath the unjust burden of retrospective taxation covering so many years. Many were even driven to make a present of their property to the informers or to the Treasury and let everything go.

In the second place, the Medes[123] and the Saracens had ravaged the greater part of Asia, and the Huns, Slavs and Antae the whole of Europe; they had razed some of the cities to the ground, and others they had utterly stripped of their wealth

119. The 'owners of the *choria*', or estate village settlements.
120. This claim is made in spite of the fact that these officials are likely to have been considerable landowners in their own right.
121. Procopius reckons Justinian's reign as having begun at Justin's accession in 518, indicating a date of composition of *c.* 550.
122. An apparent reference to what in Latin were known as the *honestiores*: members of the upper classes.
123. I.e. the Persians.

through forced levies; they had carried off the population into slavery with all their possessions and had emptied every territory of its inhabitants by their daily raids. Yet Justinian did not relieve a single man of the tax due, except that he granted captured cities exemption for one year.[124] And yet, if like the Emperor Anastasius he had decided to relieve the captured cities of all the payments due for a period of seven years, I think that even so he would have done less than he should, considering that Cabades had done the minimum damage to the buildings and then gone right away, whereas Chosroes had burned whole cities to the ground and had brought far greater misery than Cabades on those who fell in his path. To these men for whom he had made this derisory remission of taxation and to all the others – though they had often been invaded by the army of the Medes, and though the Huns and wild Saracens had continually ravaged the eastern part of the Empire, and the barbarian tribes of Europe were doing the same thing all the time and every day to the Romans in that area – the Emperor from the very first showed himself a worse enemy than all the barbarians combined.[125] For what with the requisitions,[126] and the so-called 'assignments'[127] and 'levies' for insolvent names,[128] the enemy had no sooner withdrawn than the landowners were brought to ruin. The meaning and implication of these terms I will now explain.

Those who own estate settlements are compelled to feed the Roman army in proportion to the tax levied on each landowner, the contributions being handed in not to meet the pressure of an immediate requirement but to suit the convenience and decision of the officials, who do not bother to find out whether

---

124. In 553 Justinian did, in fact, remit tax arrears (thus providing a terminus ante quem for the date of composition) whilst admitting that this was the first time he had done so: see *J.Nov.* 147.

125. Echoing the language used by Justinian to describe the harm done to taxpayers by corrupt officials in *J.Nov.* 32.

126. I.e. the *synônê*; see *Codex Iustinianus* 10.27.2, and *J.Nov.* 130.

127. I.e. the *epibolê*; see *J.Nov.* 128.

128. Known in Greek as the *diagraphê*: taxes owed by insolvent or deceased owners were reallocated amongst the other taxpayers within the fiscal districts to which they belonged. See *J.Nov.* 128 and 131.

the landowners are lucky enough to have the provisions called for in their possession. This means that these poor wretches are forced to go elsewhere to find provisions for the soldiers and fodder for the horses, buying them all at shockingly inflated prices, and that from a district which may possibly be a long way off, and then to cart them back to the place where the army happens to be. On arrival they must measure them out to the army quarter-masters, not in the universally accepted manner but rather just as the quarter-masters wish. This is the procedure known as 'requisition', the effect of which is to cripple the lords of the estates. For it compels them to pay in taxation no less than ten times the proper sum, since, as already remarked, besides contributing supplies for the army, they have often had to face the additional task of transporting grain to Byzantium. For Barsymes, as he was called, was not the only one who had dared to behave in this abominable way; before him there was the Cappadocian, and since Barsymes' time all who have followed him in his high office have been equally guilty.

This is roughly what the 'requisition' means. The term *assignment* denotes an unforeseen catastrophe that falls out of the blue on the owners of estates and puts paid to all hopes of a livelihood. In other words, it is a tax on estate properties that have been abandoned or have gone out of production, the lords and land-labourers of which have already perished altogether, or else have deserted their ancestral estates and are buried under the troubles that have come upon them as a result of these charges.[129] And they are shameless enough to impose them on anyone who has not yet gone under completely.

Such is the signification of the term *assignment*, a word that naturally was on everyone's lips at this particular time. The question of the 'levies' we may dispose of in very few words, if we put it this way. Many crushing demands, especially at this time, were showered on the cities, as was inevitable: what prompted them and what form they took I will not attempt to

---

129. Replicating the language used to describe this phenomenon (a flight from the land in response to fiscal pressure) in *J.Nov.* 80.

explain at this stage, or my account would go on forever. These demands were met by the owners of the estates, each paying an assessed sum in proportion to the tax regularly levied on him.[130] But that was not the end of their troubles: when the plague swept through the whole inhabited world and notably the Roman Empire, wiping out most of the agricultural labourers, and when as a result of this the village properties of the estates had become deserted, Justinian showed no mercy towards their lords. Even then at no point did he refrain from demanding the annual payment of tax, not only the amount at which he assessed each individual landowner but also the amount for which his deceased neighbours were liable. Beyond this they had to cope with all the other demands which I mentioned a little way back, as resting all the time on the shoulders of those who were cursed with the ownership of estates. And on top of all that, they had to vacate their best and most richly furnished rooms in order to accommodate soldiers and wait on them hand and foot, while they themselves had to live all the time in the most wretched and dilapidated hovels they possessed.[131]

Throughout the reign of Justinian and Theodora all these miseries were constantly afflicting the people, for during this time there was no respite from war or any other major calamity. And as I have referred to the vacating of rooms I must not omit to mention this fact, that owners of households in Byzantium had to provide accommodation in them for some 70,000 or so barbarians and not only could derive no satisfaction from their own property but had to put up with a great deal of other unpleasantness into the bargain.

[24] Nor can I possibly leave unrecorded Justinian's treatment of the soldiers, whom he put under the authority of the greatest scoundrels he could find, commanding these officers to rake in as much as they could from this source, on the clear understanding that a twelfth of all they managed to collect

130. Proportionality was a fixed principle of imperial fiscal practice: see *Codex Iustinianus* 10.27.2.
131. For attempts made by landowners to suborn such troops, however, see *J.Nov.* 116 and 130.

would be theirs to keep.[132] He gave them the title of 'Logothetes'. These devised the following plan, to apply year by year. It is the established custom that army pay is not given to all soldiers alike on the same scale. When the men are still young and have not been long in the ranks, the rate is lower: when they have seen active service for a while and are now halfway up the muster-roll, the pay goes up too. Finally, when they have grown old in service and are nearing the date of their discharge, the pay is much more impressive still, so that they themselves after returning to civilian life may have enough to live on for the rest of their days, and when at last their time is up they may be in a position to leave out of their own fund something to console their families. Time, in fact, is continually raising the soldiers at the foot of the ladder to the rungs vacated by those who have died or have been discharged from the forces, adjusting on the basis of seniority the pay which each man receives from public funds.

But the so-called 'Logothetes' would not permit the names of the dead to be removed from the lists, even when large numbers had died at the same time, chiefly in the constant wars. And they no longer bothered to add new names to the lists, even over a long period. The inevitable result has been that the state never has enough serving soldiers, and the soldiers that remain are kept out by others long since dead, and so are left with status much lower than their due, and receive pay at less than the proper rate, while the Logothetes constantly allot to Justinian a share of the soldiers' money.

Moreover, they impoverished the soldiers with deductions of many other kinds – a poor reward for the dangers they faced in war – reproaching some with being *Graeci*[133] (as if it was quite impossible for any man from Greece to be worthy of respect); others with being in the armed forces without having received orders from the Emperor, though on this point they could

---

132. Soldiers played an active part in tax collection; it was a standard feature for officials to derive their own stipends from such revenues as they were obliged to collect. See *J.Edict* 13 for the case of Egypt.

133. The Latin word is used contemptuously instead of the Greek *Hellenes*, which was more commonly used by this period to signify pagans.

produce a document from the Emperor's hand, which the Logothetes were impudent enough to impugn without hesitation;
and still others on the grounds that they had been absent for a
few days without leave.[134] Later some of the Palace Guards were
sent into all parts of the Empire, allegedly to scrutinize the lists
for the names of any men quite unfit for military service. For
some of these were brutal enough to strip them of their belts[135]
as a sign that the men were useless or worn out. For the rest of
their days these outcasts had to stand in public, begging charitable folk to give them something to eat, to the great distress of
all who met them. The rest they compelled to pay heavily for
the privilege of not suffering the same fate for themselves. Thus
it was that the soldiers, crippled in so many ways, became the
most poverty-stricken people in the world and lost all their
military morale.

It was this that led to the destruction of Roman power in
Italy. When Alexander the Logothete was sent there, he had the
brazen audacity to reproach the soldiers with these very things,
and he extracted money from the Italians, declaring that he was
punishing them for their policy towards Theoderic and the
Goths. And it was not only the rank and file who were reduced
to poverty and destitution by the Logothetes: the officers who
served under all the generals, a large body of men who had
previously been held in high esteem, were crushed beneath the
burden of hunger and extreme poverty. For they had no means
of providing themselves with their customary allowances.

While we are on the subject of soldiers I will add one more
thing to what I have said. The Roman Emperors before
Justinian's time stationed huge numbers of soldiers on all the
remote frontiers of the Roman Empire, particularly in the eastern region as a means of stopping the incursions of the Persians
and Saracens. These troops were called *Limitanei*. The Emperor
Justinian treated them with such indifference and niggardliness
from the start that their paymasters were four or five years in
arrears with their pay, and when peace was declared between

134. For military abscondment see *J.Nov.* 116.
135. I.e. forcibly discharge them.

the Romans and the Persians these unfortunate men, on the ground that they too would enjoy the blessings of peace, were forced to make a present to the Treasury of the pay due to them for a stated period. Later he deprived them even of the name of the soldiers without giving any reason. From then on the frontiers of the Roman Empire were left ungarrisoned, and the soldiers suddenly found themselves dependent on the generosity of those who were accustomed to charitable acts.

Other soldiers, numbering no fewer than 3,500 men, had been recruited originally to guard the Palace. These troops were known as *Scholarii*. From the start the Treasury had always rewarded them with higher pay than any of the soldiers received. The men whom the earlier Emperors enrolled in this elite corps were Armenians chosen for their merit alone, but from the accession of Zeno there was nothing to prevent the feeblest and most unwarlike specimen of humanity from gaining admission to this exclusive body. As time went on, even slaves by handing over the necessary price were able to buy the privilege of serving in it. So on Justin's accession this man Justinian admitted a shoal of candidates to this famous corps, thereby making himself a lot of money. Then, when he saw that there was not one vacancy left on this unit's muster-roll, he added the names of 2,000 additional recruits, who were known as Supernumeraries. But when he himself took over the Empire, he shook off these Supernumeraries with great speed, without giving them any money at all.

For those who belonged to the main body of the *Scholarii* he devised the following scheme. When an army was likely to be sent into Libya or Italy or against the Persians, he used to order these too to pack their baggage ready to join the expedition, though he knew perfectly well that they were quite unfit for active service. They, in terror lest this might really happen, surrendered their pay to him for a stated period. This happened to the *Scholarii* again and again. Peter too, all the time he occupied the position of *Magister*, as it is called, plagued them every day with unspeakable thefts. For though he was mild-mannered and would never dream of wronging anyone, he was the biggest thief alive, full to overflowing with sordid meanness.

This man Peter was referred to in the previous accounts as having engineered the murder of Amalasuntha, Theoderic's daughter.[136]

Besides this body of men there are others in the Palace much more highly regarded; for the Treasury always allows them a much higher rate of pay in recognition of the fact that they have paid still larger sums for the prestige attached to the service. These are known as *Domestici* and *Protectores*, and never from the start have they come within sight of an enemy: it is merely for the sake of rank and appearance that they apply for admission to the Palace Guards. For a long time now some of these have been stationed in Byzantium and some in Galatia and other places. But these like the others Justinian periodically intimidated by the method described already, compelling them to surrender their claim to the pay that was theirs by right. This can be explained in a few words. There was a law that once in five years the Emperor should bestow on every soldier a fixed sum of gold, and every fifth year they sent to all parts of the Empire and presented each soldier with five gold coins.[137] It was quite impossible ever to invent an excuse for evading this duty. Yet from the day this man took over the running of the state he has never done anything of the kind or shown any intention of doing it, although no fewer than thirty-two years have already gone by, so that this custom has been forgotten by most people.

I will now go on to describe yet another method by which he despoiled his subjects. Those who serve the Emperor and his ministers in Byzantium, either by undertaking guard duty or by handling his correspondence or in any other way, are appointed at first to the lowest ranks, and as time goes on they rise steadily to take the places of those who have died or retired, and every man rises in rank till the moment comes when he reaches the topmost rung of the ladder and arrives at last at the pinnacle of his career. Those who have reached this exalted rank are entitled by long-established custom to a salary on such a scale

136. *Wars* 5.4.17.
137. I.e. *solidi*.

that their annual income amounts to more than a hundred *centenaria* of gold, and besides being amply provided for in their old age they are as a rule in a position to make contributions from this source for the assistance of many others. As a result the business of the state has always achieved a high degree of efficiency. But this Emperor, by depriving them of nearly all of these emoluments, injured not only the officials themselves but everyone else as well. For poverty attacked them first and then went on through the rest who had hitherto enjoyed some share of their prosperity. And if anyone were to compute the loss from this source which they have had to bear for thirty-two years, he would soon arrive at the total sum of which they were so cruelly deprived.

[25] Such, then, were the ways in which this tyrant ruined those in public service. I shall now go on to relate what he did to the merchants and sailors, and to the craftsmen and market-traders and, through them, to everyone else. There are straits on both sides of Byzantium, one at the Hellespont between Sestus and Abydus, the other at the mouth of the Euxine Sea, where the place called Hieron is situated. Now at the strait on the Hellespont there had never been an official customs house, but an official sent out by the Emperor was stationed at Abydus, keeping an eye open for any ship carrying arms to Byzantium without the Emperor's leave, and for anyone setting sail from Byzantium without carrying documents and seals from the appropriate officials; for it is not permissible for anyone to sail from Byzantium till he has been cleared by the men employed in the office of the official called the *Magister*. A further duty of the Emperor's representative was to collect from the owners of the ships a toll that hurt no one but was a sort of fee which the holder of the office felt he should receive as a reward for his trouble. By contrast the man stationed at the other strait had always received his salary from the Emperor, and kept both eyes wide open for the things mentioned earlier, and for anything that was being taken to the barbarians settled along the coast of the Euxine in contravention of the regulations governing exports from the territory of the Romans to that of their enemies. But this man was

forbidden to accept anything from those whose voyages took
them that way.

Directly as Justinian took over the Empire he established
official customs houses on both straits and regularly sent out
two salaried officers. He arranged for the salaries to be paid to
them, it is true, but he impressed on them that they must use
every endeavour to see that he received as much money as
possible from their operations. The officers, having no other
ambition than to convince him of the strength of their loyalty
to him, forced the seamen to hand over the entire cash value of
their cargoes.

That was the course he followed at both straits. And in
Byzantium he thought out the following scheme. He created a
special post for one of his closest friends, a Syrian by birth
named Addaeus: he was to secure a little profit from the ships
that put in there and pass it on to his master. From then on
Addaeus never allowed any vessel that put in to the harbour
of Byzantium to weigh anchor again but either mulcted the
shipmasters of the value of their own ships or forced them to
return to Libya or Italy. Some of them declined either to accept
a return cargo or to go on seafaring any more: they preferred
to burn their boats and wash their hands of the whole business.
There were some, however, who were unable to earn their
living in any other way: their answer was to treble their charges
to the importers and take on cargoes as before. The only course
left to the importing merchants was to recoup their own losses
at the expense of those who purchased the cargoes. Thus
everything possible was being done to kill off the Romans by
starvation.

So much for that aspect of public affairs. Another subject
which I think I ought to mention is the action which the imperial
pair took with regard to the small-denomination coinage. The
money-changers had always been prepared to give their customers 210 obols (which they call *folles*)[138] in exchange for a

---

138. Copper coins: a rate of exchange that had been in place since the Emperor
      Anastasius had overhauled small-denomination coinage in the late fifth
      century.

single gold coin.[139] These two managed to line their own pockets by ordaining that only 180 obols should be given for the gold coin.[140] By this means they cut off a sixth[141] part of the value of every gold coin . . . of all men.[142]

When these rulers had put almost all commodities in the hands of the so-called 'monopolies', all the time relentlessly choking the life out of would-be customers, and only the cloth-iers' shops were left free from their clutches, they contrived a scheme for disposing of these as well. The manufacture of silken garments had for many generations been a staple industry of Beirut and Tyre, two cities of Phoenicia. The merchants who handled these and the craftsmen and artisans who produced them had lived there from time immemorial, and their wares were carried from there into every land. During Justinian's reign, those engaged in this trade in Byzantium and the other cities began to charge a higher price for dress materials of this kind, justifying themselves on the ground that they were now having to pay the Persians more for it than in the past, and that there were now more customs houses in the land of the Romans. The Emperor gave everyone to understand that he was highly displeased at this and published a law debarring anyone for charging more than eight gold pieces for a pound of this material.[143] The penalty fixed for anyone who broke this law was to forfeit all his property. The reaction of the public was to condemn this legislation as impracticable and quite unmanage-able. For it was not possible for the importers, who had bought the material in bulk at a higher price, to sell them to the dealers

139. I.e. per gold *solidus*.
140. The rate of exchange between gold and copper coinage was altered from 210 *folles* to the *solidus* to 180. This would have benefited the more humble members of society, who used the copper coinage, to the detri-ment of the state and the aristocracy, for whom gold was the unit of account. It is instructive that Procopius regarded this as a bad thing. The rate of exchange would appear to have first been altered in 538, followed by further depreciations of the gold currency.
141. Actually a seventh, but the MSS are clear on this, as is the *Suda* lexicon.
142. There is a lacuna in the text.
143. This edict no longer survives, although price controls in general are referred to in *J.Nov.* 122.

for less. The result was that they were no longer prepared to spend their energies in this traffic and proceeded to dispose of their remaining stocks by selling under the counter, presumably to certain of those well-known characters who enjoyed parading about in such finery however much it might deplete their finances, or felt it incumbent on them to do so. But when the Empress as a result of certain whispers became aware of what was going on, she did not stop to investigate the rumours but immediately stripped the owners of all their stocks, fining them a *centenaria* of gold . . .[144]

And amongst the Romans this trade is under the control of the head of the imperial finances.[145] So soon after appointing Peter Barsymes to this office they left him free to engage in any shady transaction he wished. He insisted that everyone else should obey the law to the last detail, but he forced those employed in this trade to work for his benefit alone; and without any further concealment, in full view of the people in the marketplace, he proceeded to sell dyed silk of common quality at a price of not less than six gold pieces for a single ounce, while for the imperial dye, generally known as *holoverum*, he charged more than twenty-four gold pieces. By this means he was able to hand over large sums of money to the Emperor, and to keep still more for himself without being noticed. This practice, which began with him, has continued ever since; for to this day this magistrate alone openly occupies the position of the sole importer and retailer of this merchandise.

The importers who had hitherto been occupied with this trade in Byzantium and all the other cities, whether operating on the sea or on land, naturally had to endure the hardships resulting from these operations. And in the cities referred to almost the entire population suddenly found themselves beggars. For the mechanics and craftsmen were inevitably com-

144. Lacuna.
145. I.e. the Count of the Sacred Largesses. The creation of an effective imperial monopoly in the silk trade was a great achievement of Byzantine statecraft, as high-grade silk served as a crucial commodity in diplomatic exchanges in this period with the post-Roman kingdoms to the West, and was to remain such well into the High Middle Ages.

pelled to struggle against starvation, and many in consequence abandoned the state to which they belonged and fled for refuge to the land of Persia. Year after year the whole profit from this trade came into the hands of one man, the magistrate in charge of finances, who as we have said was good enough to hand a portion of his receipts from this source back to the Emperor but secured the bulk for himself and grew rich at the cost of public misery. So much for that.

[26] How Justinian managed to destroy all the honours and public ornaments in Byzantium and every city besides will be our next subject. First he decided to lower the status of the professional lawyers, and speedily deprived them of all the rewards which had hitherto enabled them to live in luxury and elegance when their work in the courts was done, ordering the litigants to take oaths and settle their disputes for themselves.[146] As a result of this contemptuous treatment the legal profession fell into great despondency. And after he deprived the members of the Senate and everybody else who was regarded as prosperous, either in Byzantium or in any other city, of all their property, as we have already seen, the legal profession was left unemployed. For people possessed nothing of the least value to go to court about.[147] So in a very little while, their once great numbers and dazzling reputation shrank to vanishing point everywhere, and inevitably they were reduced to penury and ended by getting nothing for their labours except insults.[148]

Again, he caused doctors and the teachers of gentlemen's sons to go short of the elementary necessities of life. For the stipends which earlier Emperors ordered to be issued to members of these professions Justinian took away altogether.

---

146. I.e. Justinian preferred dispute settlement by arbitration and negotiation rather than litigation: see the epilogue to *J.Nov.* 112. A considerable number of dispute settlements (Greek *dialyseis*) survive in the documentary papyri from sixth-century Egypt. Justinian also sought to curtail the opportunity for litigants to pursue their cases through a series of appeal courts through to Constantinople: see *J.Nov.* 23.

147. Justinian decreed that cases relating to sums of less than 500 *solidi* (later raised to 720 gold coins) were disbarred from consideration by the higher courts of appeal: see *J.Nov.* 24–31 and 103.

148. Procopius is, of course, writing as a lawyer.

Moreover, the whole of the revenues which all the inhabitants of the cities had raised locally for communal purposes and for entertainments he took over and shamelessly pooled with the revenues of the central government. From then on doctors and teachers counted for nothing: no one was now in a position to plan any public building projects; no lamps were lit in the streets of the cities; and there was nothing else to make life pleasant for city-dwellers. Theatres, hippodromes and circuses were almost all shut – the very places where his wife had been born and brought up, and had received her early training. Later on, he gave orders that all these places of entertainment should be closed down in Byzantium, to save the Treasury from having to finance the payments hitherto made to the people – so numerous that I cannot estimate their numbers – who depended on them for a living. Both in private and in public there was grief and dejection, as if yet another visitation from heaven had struck them, and all laughter had gone out of life. People discussed no subject whatever, whether they were at home or meeting each other in the market-place or passing a few moments in places of worship, other than calamities and miseries, and a great mass of novel misfortunes.

Such was the state of affairs in the cities. And what remains to be narrated also deserves to be told. Two Roman consuls were appointed every year, one in Rome, the other in Byzantium. Whoever was honoured with this office was bound to expend for official purposes more than twenty *centenaria* of gold, a little of this being drawn from his own resources, the bulk from the Emperor. This money was normally handed over to those I have mentioned and to those who were exceptionally short of means, and especially to those associated with the stage, thereby providing constant support for all civic affairs. But since Justinian's acquisition of imperial power these measures were no longer taken at the proper time: at first a Roman consul was appointed very belatedly, but in the end such an appointment was never seen even in a dream,[149] so that unfortunate mortals were perpetually in the grip of virtual

149. Justinian moth-balled the consulship in 541; see *J.Nov.* 105.

penury, as the Emperor no longer provided his subjects with the customary subventions but everywhere and in every way stripped them of the little they had.

Now I have said enough, I think, to make clear how this destroyer has swallowed up all the funds of the state and has stripped all the members of the Senate, both individually and collectively, of their possessions. I think too that I have given an adequate description of the way in which by employing blackmail he succeeded in getting a grip on all the others who were believed to be prosperous, thereby stripping them of their property – soldiers, civil servants, those who serve in the Palace, agricultural labourers, landowners and lords, practising advocates – and again, importers, shipowners and sailors, mechanics and manual labourers, and market traders, and those who make their living from the life of the stage; and yet again, pretty well all the others who are affected by the damage done to these.

Next we must speak of beggars[150] and the common people, of the poor and those suffering from various physical disabilities, and what he did to all these: his treatment of the priests will be described in a subsequent account.[151] First, as already stated, he took possession of all the shops and created so-called 'monopolies' of the most necessary commodities, forcing everyone to pay more than three times the proper price. The other things that he did seem to me beyond enumeration, and I would not attempt to list them even in an account of unlimited length. He penalized without respite or mercy the consumers of bread – manual labourers, the poor and those suffering from various physical disabilities – who must buy bread or starve. For in order to bring in from this source up to three *centenaria* a year, he arranged for the loaves to be made not only smaller but full of ash; for not even to such a monstrous display of shameless covetousness as this did this Emperor hesitate to resort. And using this as a pretext for finding means to fill their own pockets, those who administered these arrangements found it very easy to enrich themselves quite handsomely, while they brought

150. See *J.Nov.* 80.
151. Another reference to a supposed *Ecclesiastical History*.

upon the poor an artificial shortage that seemed impossible at a time of such abundance; for the importing of corn from elsewhere was strictly forbidden, and everyone was compelled to buy and eat these loaves.[152]

The city's aqueduct was broken and was carrying only a fraction of the usual quantity of water into the city. But they took no notice and would not spend any money whatsoever on it, though there was always a great crowd of people round the fountains with their tongues hanging out,[153] and all the public baths were closed. Yet he lavished money inexcusably on buildings along the shore and other senseless erections, littering all the suburbs with them, as if there was not room for him and his consort in the palaces in which all his predecessors had been happy to spend their whole lives. Thus it was not the desire to save money but the set purpose of destroying his fellow-men that led him to neglect the rebuilding of the aqueduct; for no one who has ever lived at any period of human history has been more ready than Justinian to pile up wealth by immoral means and instantly squander it in still more shocking ways. By way of food and drink only two things, then, were left to those who were utterly destitute – bread and water; and the Emperor, as I have already made clear, employed both of these to make life impossible for them by making the one more costly, the other quite unobtainable.

It was not only the beggars in Byzantium but also some who lived elsewhere who suffered thus at his hands, as I shall relate forthwith. When Theoderic had overrun Italy, he let the armed guard in the palace at Rome remain where it was, so that some trace of the ancient constitution might be preserved there, leaving a small daily wage for each man. These men were very numerous; they included the so-called *Silentarii* and *Domestici* and *Scholarii*, who had nothing left to them but the name of

152. Feeding the population of Constantinople posed formidable logistical challenges: thus the state's channelling of the Egyptian corn supply to meet the city's needs.

153. Possibly 'in a state of indignation'. As with food, providing the city with a secure water supply was no mean feat, necessitating the construction and maintenance of a cat's cradle of aqueducts and reservoirs.

soldiers and this pay (which was hardly enough to keep body and soul together): these two things were to be passed on to their children and descendants. To the beggars who spent their days in the shadow of the Church of the Apostle Peter, he instructed the Treasury to distribute every year 3,000 measures of corn.[154] This allowance all these men continued to receive until the arrival of Alexander the Clipper,[155] who without the slightest hesitation made up his mind at once to strip these unfortunates of all their perquisites. When he heard about this, Justinian, Emperor of the Romans, expressed approval of this action and held Alexander in still higher regard than before. On this journey Alexander had also victimized the Greeks, as will now appear.

The guard-post at Thermopylae had for many years been in the care of those who worked the land of the village properties there, and who took turns in guarding the wall there whenever an incursion of one barbarian tribe or another into the Peloponnese seemed imminent. But when Alexander arrived there on this occasion, he pretended to be rendering a service to the Peloponnesians by declining to leave this guard-post to be manned by agricultural labourers. So he stationed regular soldiers there to the number of 2,000 and arranged that their pay should not be provided from the imperial Treasury, but rather he diverted to the Treasury all the civic and entertainment funds of all the cities of Greece on this pretext: that they would be used to provide stipends for these soldiers. The result was that nowhere in Greece, not even in Athens itself, was any public building restored, nor could any other improvement be made. Justinian nevertheless lost no time in confirming the Clipper's activities in Greece.

So much for events in that country. Now we must turn our attention to the poor of Alexandria. Among the local lawyers there was one Hephaestus, who on being made governor of the city put a stop to public rioting by making himself an object

154. Greek *medimnoi*: one *medimonos* (Latin *modius*) was equal to one peck, or nine metric litres.
155. A Logothete who was reputed to be able to save money by imperceptibly clipping the edges of gold coins.

of dread amongst the faction members but who nevertheless brought upon the inhabitants the worst of the worst miseries. He started by bringing all the shops of the city under a so-called 'monopoly', forbidding any other merchant to carry on this business, and establishing himself as the one and only purveyor of goods. Then he began selling commodities of every kind, fixing their prices, it goes without saying, by the authority of his office, so that the city of Alexandria, where hitherto even the very poorest had found everything cheap enough to buy, was brought to the brink by the scarcity of necessities. They felt the pinch most of all through his manipulation of the bread supply, for he kept all the purchasing of grain from Egypt entirely in his own hands, allowing nobody else to buy or sell so much as a single measure: in this way he controlled the supply of bread and the price of a loaf just as he wished.[156] So he soon amassed unheard-of wealth himself and at the same time satisfied the demands of the Emperor in this matter. The people of Alexandria through fear of Hephaestus endured their sufferings in silence, and the Emperor, out of respect for the money that was all the time replenishing his coffers, was overwhelmed with love for the man.

This man Hephaestus, seeking ways of ingratiating himself still further with the Emperor, devised this additional scheme. When Diocletian had become Roman Emperor, he had arranged for a large quantity of corn to be provided yearly by the Treasury as a gift to the needy in Alexandria. From the start the inhabitants of the city shared this out amongst themselves, and they passed on the tradition to their descendants right down to now. But from the day he took office, Hephaestus robbed those who lacked the barest necessities of life of as much as 2,000,000 measures a year, putting it in government warehouses, and informing the Emperor by letter that up to then these people had been receiving the corn without any justification and without regard for the interests of the state. As a result, the Emperor endorsed his action and gave him still more enthusiastic support, while those of the Alexandrians who

156. See *J.Edict* 13 for the administration of Alexandria and the grain supply.

had no other hope of a livelihood suffered most terribly from the effects of this inhumanity.

[27] The deeds of Justinian were so many that eternity itself would not suffice for the telling of them. It will be enough for me to pick out from the long list and set down a few examples by which his whole character will be made crystal clear to men as yet unborn – what a dissembler he was, and how little he cared for God or priests or laws, or for the people to whom he professed to be so devoted, or again for any decency at all, or the interest of the state or anything that might be to its advantage. He did not attempt to make his actions seem excusable, nor did anything count with him except this alone – the seizure of all the wealth in the world. I begin with this.

As chief priest[157] of Alexandria he nominated a man called Paul. It happened that one Rhodon, Phoenician by birth, was at that time Governor of Alexandria, and the Emperor instructed him to assist Paul in all his undertakings to the limit of his power, so that not a single order issued by him might remain unfulfilled. By this means he thought he would be able to persuade the priests[158] of the Alexandrians to adhere to the Council of Chalcedon.[159] There was a native of Palestine, by name Arsenius, who had been useful to the Empress Theodora in the most important matters, and had thereby made himself very powerful and extremely rich, though his character was of the basest. This man was a Samaritan, but to avoid losing the power he now held he had to call himself a Christian. His father and brother, on the other hand, putting their trust in his power, had remained at Scythopolis, clinging to their ancestral religion and at his suggestion treating all Christians with shocking cruelty. As a result the inhabitants of the city revolted against them and put them both to the most miserable death, causing a train of disasters to befall the people of Palestine. At the same

157. I.e. Patriarch.
158. Only a suggested supplement but a more probable one than Haury's 'heretics' (accepted by Williamson) given Procopius' distinctly unpartisan approach to Christological matters.
159. The Christological formula established at Chalcedon in 451 was bitterly opposed by the Patriarchs of Alexandria and Antioch.

time he met with no retribution at the hands of either Justinian or Theodora, although he was fully responsible for all these troubles, but they forbade him to come to the Palace any more, for the stream of protests by the Christians about his behaviour left them no peace.

To get himself into the Emperor's good books, Arsenius soon afterwards set off with Paul for Alexandria, to assist him generally and in particular to do all in his power to co-operate with him in bringing the Alexandrians into line.[160] For he affirmed that, during the time when he had been unlucky enough to be debarred from entering the Palace, he made himself thoroughly familiar with all the doctrines of the Christians. This annoyed Theodora, for she kept up a pretence of going against the Emperor in doctrinal matters, as I have stated previously. So when the two men arrived in Alexandria, Paul handed over to Rhodon a deacon named Psoes to be executed, alleging that it was Psoes alone who prevented him from fulfilling the Emperor's wishes. Rhodon in obedience to the Emperor's written instructions, which came thick and fast and were most peremptory, decided to torture the man: he was stretched on the rack and died at once.

When this came to the Emperor's ears, under the strongest pressure from the Empress he at once set everything in motion against Paul, Rhodon and Arsenius, as if he had entirely forgotten the directives which he had sent to the three of them. He appointed Liberius,[161] a Patrician of Rome, Governor of Alexandria and dispatched several eminent priests to Alexandria to investigate the situation. These included the Archdeacon of Rome, Pelagius, representing the Archpriest[162] Vigilius, who had given him full authority to do so. Paul was convicted of the

160. I.e. with the Emperor's pro-Chalcedonian doctrinal views.
161. An extraordinary figure, Liberius held office in the civil service under the usurper Odoacer before defecting to Theoderic's colours. Under Theoderic he pursued a distinguished and glorious career, before defecting to the Eastern Empire while on embassy to Constantinople. After governing Alexandria, he was sent to govern the reconquered island of Sicily, and may have ended his days, a very old man, leading the Byzantine army of reconquest into Visigothic Spain.
162. I.e. Pope.

homicide and at once removed from holy orders. Rhodon fled to Byzantium and was beheaded by the Emperor, who confiscated all his property to the Treasury, although he produced thirteen letters which the Emperor had written to him, adjuring and commanding him to assist Paul in everything he wished done, and in no circumstances to go against him, so that he should be able to carry out the Emperor's wishes concerning doctrine. Arsenius, at the resolve of Theodora, was impaled by Liberius, and the Emperor decided to confiscate his property, though he had no charge to bring against him except his association with Paul.

Whether he was justified or not in taking these steps it is not for me to say, but the reason why I have described these incidents I shall make clear at once. A little later Paul came to Byzantium and offered the Emperor seven *centenaria* of gold with a request that he might be reinstated in his priesthood, on the grounds that he had been illegally deprived of it. Justinian received the money graciously and treated the man with great respect, agreeing to make him Archpriest of Alexandria immediately,[163] although another now occupied the position – as if he did not know that he himself had executed those who had lived with Paul and had dared to assist him, and had deprived them of their possessions. So the *Augustus*[164] flung himself into the scheme with enthusiasm and exerted himself to the utmost, and Paul was confidently expected to get back his priesthood by hook or by crook. But Vigilius, who was in Byzantium at the time, flatly refused to yield to the Emperor if he should issue such instructions: he declared that it was impossible for him to reverse his own decision – meaning the verdict given by Pelagius. So it is, then, that nothing ever mattered to this Emperor but laying his hands on other people's property. Let us look at another such episode.

There was a certain Faustinus, a native of Palestine. He was a Samaritan by descent but had become a nominal Christian under pressure from the law. This Faustinus had attained the

163. In contravention of his own legislation: see *J.Nov.* 6, 123 and 137.
164. I.e. Emperor.

rank of senator and had become governor of the region, but he
was soon removed from office and proceeded to Byzantium,
where some of the priests denounced him, alleging that he had
treated the Christians resident in Palestine atrociously. Justinian
appeared to be very angry and highly indignant at the thought
that while he was ruling over the Roman Empire the name of
Christ should be insulted by anyone. So the Senate inquired
into the matter and under heavy pressure from the Emperor
sentenced Faustinus to exile. But as soon as the Emperor had
got out of him all the money that he wanted, he rescinded the
judgement. Faustinus, restored to his former dignities, was on
easy terms with the Emperor, who appointed him overseer of
the imperial estates in Palestine and Phoenicia. There he was
able to do whatever he liked with no fear now for the consequences. Of the methods, then, by which Justinian chose to
defend the claims of the Christians we have not said very much:
but even from this brief account it will be easy to draw a
conclusion. Now it will be revealed as succinctly as possible
how, without any hesitation, he trampled on the laws when
money was in question.

[28] There was one Priscus in the city of Emesa, who was
remarkably skilled at imitating other people's handwriting and
was a most accomplished artist at this mischievous occupation.
It happened that many years earlier the church of Emesa had
been made the heir of one of the notables. This man was of
Patrician rank, and his name was Mammianus, and he was a
man of very distinguished birth and of immense wealth. During
Justinian's reign Priscus investigated all the families of the city
we have named, and if he found any persons who were very
well off and able to survive the loss of large sums, he would
trace their progenitors with great care, and if he could put his
hand on any old letters of theirs, he forged documents pur-
porting to have been written by them. In these they promised
to pay Mammianus large sums which they were supposed to
have received from him in return for a mortgage. The amount
of money acknowledged in these forged documents totalled not
less than a hundred *centenaria*. At the time when Mammianus
was still alive there was a man with a great reputation for

honesty and other virtues who used to sit in the marketplace raising all the inhabitants' documents and countersigning each one himself in his own handwriting. The Romans call such a man a *tabellio*. Priscus made a magically clever imitation of this man's writing and handed the documents to the estate administrators of the church in Emesa, in return for a promise that a share of the money that they expected to collect from that source should be reserved for him.

But the law barred the way, for it laid down a thirty-year limitation for all ordinary claims, the period being extended to forty years in a few cases, particularly those arising from mortgages.[165] So they contrived the following scheme. They came to Byzantium and paid a great deal of money to this Emperor, begging him to co-operate with them in engineering the ruin of their completely innocent compatriots. He gathered up the money, and in the twinkling of an eye he had promulgated a law to the effect that churches should be allowed to prosecute their claims not only during the statutory period but for a full hundred years. This regulation was to hold good not only in Emesa but throughout the entire Roman Empire.[166] To supervise the new system in Emesa he nominated Longinus, a man of action and of splendid physique, who later became the magistrate set in charge of the populace of Byzantium.[167] The administrators of the church's estates began by lodging a claim for two *centenaria*, on the basis of the documents mentioned, against one of the city's inhabitants. They soon obtained judgement against this unfortunate man, who was quite incapable of putting up a defence because so much time had elapsed, and he knew nothing about what had happened at the time in question. Being equally at the mercy of the informers, all his fellow Emesenes were distressed beyond measure, especially the most notable amongst them.

When this mischief was already sweeping over the majority of the inhabitants of the city, the Providence of God intervened

165. A period of limitation for claims established by Theodosius II in 424.
166. See *J. Nov.* 9 and 111.
167. I.e. the Urban Prefect of Constantinople.

opportunely as follows. Longinus commanded Priscus, the author of this scam, to bring him the whole collection of documents, and when he declined to do so Longinus struck him as hard as he could. Priscus, unable to stand up to the blow of so powerful a man, fell flat on his back, and – trembling now and overcome with terror, and suspecting that Longinus knew all about what had been going on – he made a clean breast of it. Thus all his knavery was brought to light, and his efforts as an informer came to an end.

This constant and daily interference with the laws of the Romans was not all that the Emperor did: he also did his best to abolish the laws reverenced by the Hebrews. Whenever the returning months happened to bring the Passover feast before that kept by the Christians, he would not permit the Jews to celebrate this at the proper time, nor to offer anything to God at this feast, nor to perform any of their customary ceremonies. Many of them were brought to trial by those appointed governors and charged with an offence against the laws of the state, in that they had eaten lamb at this period. They were then sentenced to pay heavy fines. Justinian was guilty of innumerable other acts of this type: but though I know all about them, I shall not include any of them in this narrative, which must shortly be brought to an end. The incidents already recorded will suffice to reveal the man's character only too clearly.

[29] Next I will show what a dissembling hypocrite he was. The Liberius whom I have just mentioned was dismissed from the office that he held and replaced by an Egyptian, John Laxarion. When this became known to Pelagius, who was a very intimate friend of Liberius, he asked the Emperor whether the report concerning Laxarion was correct. Justinian flatly denied it, assuring him that he had done no such thing, and he handed him a letter to Liberius, instructing him to hold on to his office most resolutely and in no circumstances to relinquish it: for he had no intention, he said, of relieving him of it for the moment.

But John had an uncle in Byzantium called Eudaemon, who had attained the rank of consul and had made a great deal of money, becoming for a time overseer of the private imperial estates.[168] When Eudaemon heard the story, he in turn asked the Emperor whether his nephew had been definitely appointed to the governorship. Justinian, denying all knowledge of the letter he had written to Liberius, wrote a letter to John instructing him to take possession of his office and to brook no interference: he himself had no second thoughts about the matter. Taking these statements at their face value, John ordered Liberius to vacate his official quarters, as he had been relieved of his post. Liberius emphatically refused to accept his orders, he too relying of course on the letter he had received from the Emperor. John then armed his followers and went for Liberius, and Liberius with his own entourage took steps to defend himself. And a fight ensued and many lost their lives, including John himself, the holder of the office.

After urgent representations from Eudaemon, Liberius was instantly summoned to Byzantium, where the Senate, after making a thorough investigation of the case, acquitted him, as he had not been the aggressor but had been defending himself when this dreadful thing had happened. The Emperor, however, did not allow the matter to drop until he had secretly forced him to pay a heavy fine.

Such was Justinian's notion of truth-telling and straightforwardness. And I think it would be to the point if I mentioned the sequel to this story. Eudaemon died soon after, leaving a host of relations but making no will and giving no instructions whatsoever. About the same time, a fellow by the name of Euphratas, who had been in charge of the Palace eunuchs, departed this life, leaving a nephew but making no arrangements for the disposal of his estate, which was of exceptional size. Both these estates the Emperor seized for himself, making himself the heir of his own volition and sparing not a copper for any of the lawful heirs. Such was the respect that this Emperor showed for the laws of the land and for the kinsfolk of his closest friends! In just the same way he had seized the

168. 'Count of the Private Property' (Latin *comes rei privatae*).

property of Irenaeus, who had died at a much earlier date, though he had no claim to it whatever.

Another episode that was connected with these incidents and took place at about the same time deserves mention. There was a man called Anatolius who held chief place on the list of precedence of the city councillors in Ascalon. His daughter had become wife to an inhabitant of Caesarea, by name Mamilian, a man of very distinguished aristocratic lineage. The girl was an heiress, as Anatolius had no other child. Now it was laid down by an ancient law that whenever a councillor[169] of any of the cities departed this life without male issue, one quarter of his estate should be given to the city council, while the next of kin of the deceased enjoyed all the remainder. Here too the Emperor showed his true character. For he happened to have recently promulgated a law which reversed everything. From then on, whenever a city councillor died leaving no male issue, the next of kin were to share the quarter of the estate while all the rest went to the Treasury and to the account of the city council.[170] And yet never before in the history of mankind had Treasury or Emperor been permitted to share in the property of city councillors.

After this law came into force, Anatolius reached the end of his days, and his daughter divided the estate with the Treasury and the city council in accordance with the law. Both the Emperor himself and those who maintained the register of city councillors in Ascalon wrote letters to her indemnifying her against any claim on her share, as they had duly and justly received what belonged to them. Later on, Mamilian too departed this life, the son-in-law of the late Anatolius, leaving only one child – a daughter – who naturally received the whole of her father's estate. Later, while her mother was still alive, she too passed away. She had been married to one of the notables but had borne no children male or female. Justinian promptly grabbed the lot, voicing the extraordinary opinion that the daughter of Anatolius was now an old woman, and

169. Greek *bouleutês* or Latin *curialis*. For the law, see *Codex Iustinianus*
    10.35.1.
170. A distorted reading of *J.Nov.* 38.

that for her to grow rich on both her husband's and her father's money would be quite immoral. But in order that the woman might not have to join the ranks of the beggars, he arranged for her to receive a gold coin a day for the rest of her life, finding room in the document by which he purloined all this money for a declaration that he was sacrificing the coin for the sake of piety: 'For it is my custom,' he said, 'to do what is pious and righteous.'

But on this subject I have said enough. I do not wish to bore my readers, and in any case no man alive could recount all that Justinian did on these lines. I will next make clear that he never had any regard even for the Blues, to whom he expressed so much devotion, if there was money to be had. In Cilicia there was one Malthanes, son-in-law to that Leo who, as I mentioned earlier, held the office of *Referendarius*. To this man Justinian gave the duty of suppressing the acts of violence in Cilicia. Seizing on this pretext, Malthanes did untold damage to most of the Cilicians, plundering their property and sending some of it to the tyrant, while he unscrupulously enriched himself with the rest. Most of them bore their miseries in silence, but those inhabitants of Tarsus who were Blues, presuming on the liberty allowed them by the Emperor, showered public insults on Malthanes when he was not there to hear them. But he soon knew all about it, and at the head of a large body of soldiers went straight to Tarsus in the night. Immediately before dawn he sent his men to the houses on every side, ordering them to quarter themselves there. Thinking this to be an armed raid, the Blues put up what defence they could. In the darkness much damage was done; in particular Damian, a city councillor, was struck by an arrow and killed.

This Damian had been patron of the Blues there, and when his death became known in Byzantium the Blues were furious and made an uproarious tumult in the city, protesting to the Emperor about the incident and giving him no peace, and excoriating Leo and Malthanes with terrifying threats. The Emperor pretended to be just as indignant at what had happened. He at once wrote a letter ordering that Malthanes' conduct of his public duties be investigated and punished. But

Leo presented him with a handsome quantity of gold, where-upon both his wrath and his affection for the Blues vanished in a moment. While the matter remained uninvestigated, Malthanes came to Byzantium to see the Emperor, who welcomed him in the most friendly manner and treated him as a distinguished visitor. But as he came away from the Emperor's presence, the Blues, who had been waiting for him, showered blows on him in the Palace, and would have finished him off had they not been restrained by some of their number who happened to have been secretly bribed by Leo already.

Could anything be imagined more wretched than a state in which an Emperor accepted a bribe to leave accusations uninvestigated, and factionists, while the Emperor was in his Palace, did not hesitate or scruple to rise up against one of the governors and make an unjustifiable attack on him? Yet no punishment for these crimes ever came the way of either Malthanes or his assailants. From these facts, if anyone should wish to do so, it would be easy to estimate the character of the Emperor Justinian.

[30] Whether Justinian cared anything for the welfare of the state is made plain enough by the way in which he treated the Public Post and the intelligence officers. The Roman Emperors of earlier days took precautions to ensure that everything should be reported to them instantly and should be subject to no delay – such things as damage inflicted by the enemy on this region or that, trouble in the cities caused by faction fights or by some other unexpected disaster, and the actions of governors and all the other officials in every part of the Roman Empire. Secondly, they were anxious that those who conveyed the yearly tax revenues to the capital should arrive there safely without danger or delay. With these two objects in view they organized a swift public postal service in all directions. The method was this. Within the distance that a man lightly equipped might be expected to cover in a day they established stations, on some roads eight, on others fewer, but very rarely less than five. As many as forty horses stood ready at each station, and grooms corresponding to the number of horses were installed at every station. Always as they rode the professional couriers changed

their horses – which were most carefully chosen – at frequent intervals, and covering, if occasion required, a ten-day journey in a single day, they performed all the services I have just described. Moreover, the lords of the land everywhere, especially if their estate properties happened to be a long way from the coast, derived great benefit from this system, for every year they sold the surplus of their crops to the government to provide food for both horses and grooms, and thus made lots of money. So it was that the Treasury could rely on receiving the tax due from every taxpayer, while those who paid the money got it back again immediately, and into the bargain the needs of the state were met.

This had been the state of affairs hitherto. But this Emperor began by dismantling the postal service from Chalcedon to Daciviza, forcing the couriers to go all the way from Byzantium to Helenopolis by sea, much as they objected. So they make the journey in tiny boats of the kind normally used for crossing the strait, and if a storm happens to fall on them they run into serious danger. For since it is their duty to make the utmost haste, any holding back for the right moment or waiting for a hoped-for calm is ruled out. Secondly, on the road leading to Persia he did allow the postal service to continue according to the established plan, but on all other eastward routes as far as Egypt he laid down that there should be only one station for each day's journey, and that furnished not with horses but with a small number of asses. The result has been that events happening in any region are reported with difficulty, too late to be of any use and long after they have happened, so that naturally no effective action can be taken, and the owners of fields, seeing their own crops rotting and going to waste, are rendered perpetually profitless.

And with the intelligence officers it is as follows. From the first, many men were employed in the service of the state. They used to venture forth into enemy territory and contrive an entry into the palace of the Persians,[171] under cover either of trade or some other ruse. Then, after making careful note of everything,

---

171. At Ctesiphon, near modern Baghdad.

they came back into the land of the Romans and were in a position to acquaint the Emperor's ministers with all the secrets of the enemy. The ministers, warned in advance, kept up their guard and were never taken unawares. This system had been in use amongst the Medes also since ancient times. Chosroes, in fact, so they say, raised the pay of his intelligence officers and benefited by his foresight. For nothing [that was happening among the Romans escaped] him, [whereas Justinian by refusing to spend a penny on them] blotted out [the very] name of intelligence officers from the dominions of Rome.[172] This folly was the cause of many mistakes, and Lazica fell to the enemy, the Romans being completely in the dark as to the whereabouts of the Persian Emperor and his army.

But that was not the limit of his folly. For a very long time the state had regularly maintained great numbers of camels, which followed the Roman army as it advanced towards an enemy and carried everything the army required. There was no compulsion on the land-labourers to provide corvée services, nor did the soldiers ever go short of necessities. But Justinian did away with nearly all of these too. Consequently when the Roman army of today advances against the enemy, its movements are severely restricted.

That, then, is the way things were going with the most pressing concerns of the state. But it would not be amiss to add a word about one of Justinian's more ridiculous actions. Among the practising lawyers at Caesarea was one Evangelus, a man who had made a considerable mark. The wind of Fortune had blown so favourably for him that he acquired property of many kinds and had become the owner of much land. And later on he even bought a large coastal village called Porphyreon, for which he paid three *centenaria* of gold. When news of this transaction reached Justinian, he promptly sequestrated the private property, giving the unfortunate man only a fraction of the price he had paid for it, and solemnly declaring that it would never be proper for a mere lawyer like Evangelus to be

172. There is a gap in the Greek text which editors have filled in various ways. Here Haury's suggestion is used.

the master of so large a town. But having touched on these matters in this summary way, I will say no more about them.

Among the innovations which Justinian and Theodora made in the conduct of government are the following. In previous reigns, when the Senate came into the Emperor's presence it was customary to do obeisance in this way. A man of Patrician rank used to salute him on the right breast: the Emperor responded by kissing him on the head and then dismissed him. Everyone else bent his right knee to the Emperor and then retired. To the Empress, however, obeisance was never paid. But when they came into the presence of Justinian and Theodora, all of them, including those who held Patrician rank, had to fall on the floor flat on their faces, stretch out their hands and feet as far as they could, touch with their lips one foot of each of the imperial pair and then stand up again. For Theodora too was disinclined to forego this sign of esteem, and even claimed the privilege of receiving the ambassadors of the Persians and of the other barbarians, and of bestowing gifts of money on them, as if the Roman Empire lay subject to her – a thing unprecedented in the whole course of history.

Again, in the past persons engaged in conversations with the Emperor called him 'Emperor' and his wife 'Empress', and addressed each of the officials by the title appropriate to the rank he held at the moment; but if anyone were to engage in conversation with either of these two and refer to the 'Emperor' or 'Empress' and not call them 'Master' and 'Mistress', or attempted to speak of any of the ministers as anything but 'slaves', he would be regarded as ignorant and impertinent, and – as if he had committed a shocking offence and deliberately insulted the last person who should have been so treated – he was sent packing.

Lastly, while in earlier reigns few visited the Palace, and they on rare occasions, from the day that these two assumed imperial power officials and people of every sort spent their days in the Palace with hardly a break. The reason was that in the old days the officials were allowed to do what was just and proper in accordance with their individual judgements; this meant that while carrying out their official duties they stayed in their own offices, while his subjects, neither seeing nor hearing of any injurious treatment, naturally troubled the Emperor very rarely. These two, however, all the time taking everything into their own hands to the detriment of their subjects, compelled everyone to be in constant attendance exactly like slaves. Almost any day one could see all the law-courts pretty well deserted, and at the Emperor's court an insolent crowd, elbowing and shoving, and all the time displaying the most abject servility. Those who were supposed to be close to the imperial pair stood there right through the whole day and invariably for a considerable part of the night, getting no sleep or food at the normal times, till they were practically on their last legs: this was all that their supposed good fortune brought them.

When, however, they were released from all this, the poor wretches would engage in bitter quarrels as to what had happened to the wealth of the Romans. For some insisted that it was all with the barbarians; others declared that the Emperor kept it locked up in a vast array of hideaways. Anyway, whenever Justinian, if he is a man, departs from this life, or, as the Chief of the Demons, sets this mortal life aside, then all those who have the fortune still to be alive will know the truth . . .

Further Reading

TEXT

Haury, J., *Procopius, Opera Omnia*, 3 vols (Leipzig: 1905–13); rev. G. Wirth, Teubner Series, 4 vols (Leipzig: Teubner, 1962–4). Vol. 3 of the Haury-Wirth edition (1963) contains the *Secret History*

TRANSLATIONS

Dewing, H. B., *Procopius, Works*, Loeb Classical Library, 7 vols (New York and London: Harvard University Press, 1914–35). Based on Haury's Greek text, which is reprinted with English translation on facing page. Vol. 6 (1935) contains the *Secret History*

STUDIES

Cameron, A., *Procopius and the Sixth Century* (London: Duckworth, 1985)
Kaldellis, A., *Procopius of Caesarea: Tyranny, History, and Philosophy at the End of Antiquity* (Philadelphia: University of Pennsylvania Press, 2004)

SECONDARY MATERIALS

Brown, P. R. L., *The World of Late Antiquity* (London: Thames and Hudson, 1971)
Collins, R., *Early Medieval Europe* (London: Macmillan, 1992)
Evans, J. A. S., *The Age of Justinian: The Circumstances of Imperial Power* (London: Routledge, 1996)

Maas, M. (ed.), *The Cambridge Companion to the Age of Justinian* (Cambridge: Cambridge University Press, 2005)

Mango, C., *Byzantium: The Empire of New Rome* (London: Weidenfeld & Nicolson, 1980)

Sarris, P., *Economy and Society in the Age of Justinian* (Cambridge: Cambridge University Press, 2006)

Chronology

the Goths have retaken Rome; consulship abolished; bubonic plague reaches Egypt from Africa

542 Procopius witnesses the arrival of the plague in Constantinople

c. **545** Procopius begins writing the *History of the Wars*

548 Death of Theodora

548–9 Date of completion of *History of the Wars* 1–4

550 Date of composition of the *Secret History*

551 Date of completion of *History of the Wars* 5–7

553–4 Final defeat of the Ostrogoths; date of completion of *History of the Wars* 8

558 Conquest of Visigothic Spain initiated; collapse of dome of Hagia Sophia

562–3 Procopius Prefect of Constantinople?; possible approximate date of composition of the *Buildings*

565 Death of Justinian

GENEALOGICAL TABLE

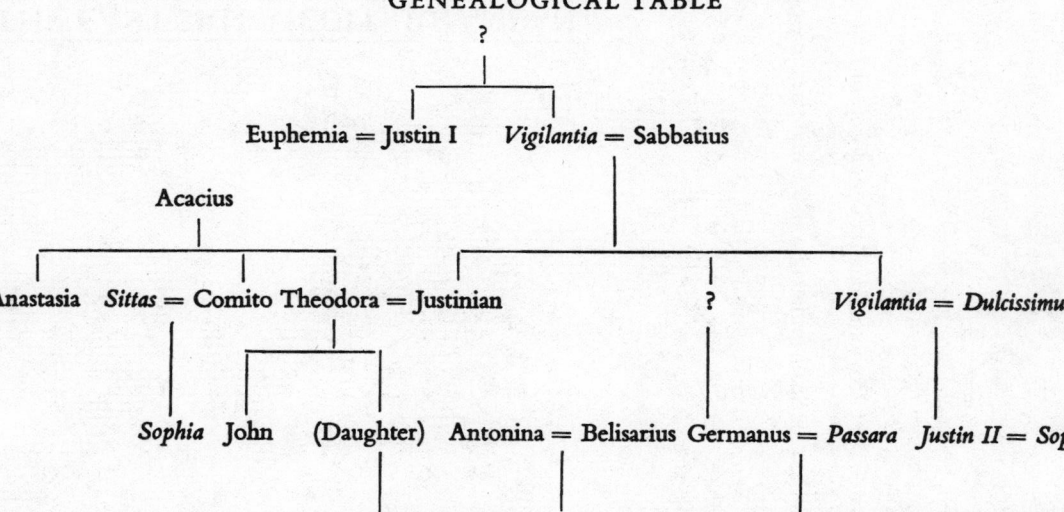

Names in italics are not found in *The Secret History*
We do not know who fathered Theodora's children or her grandchild

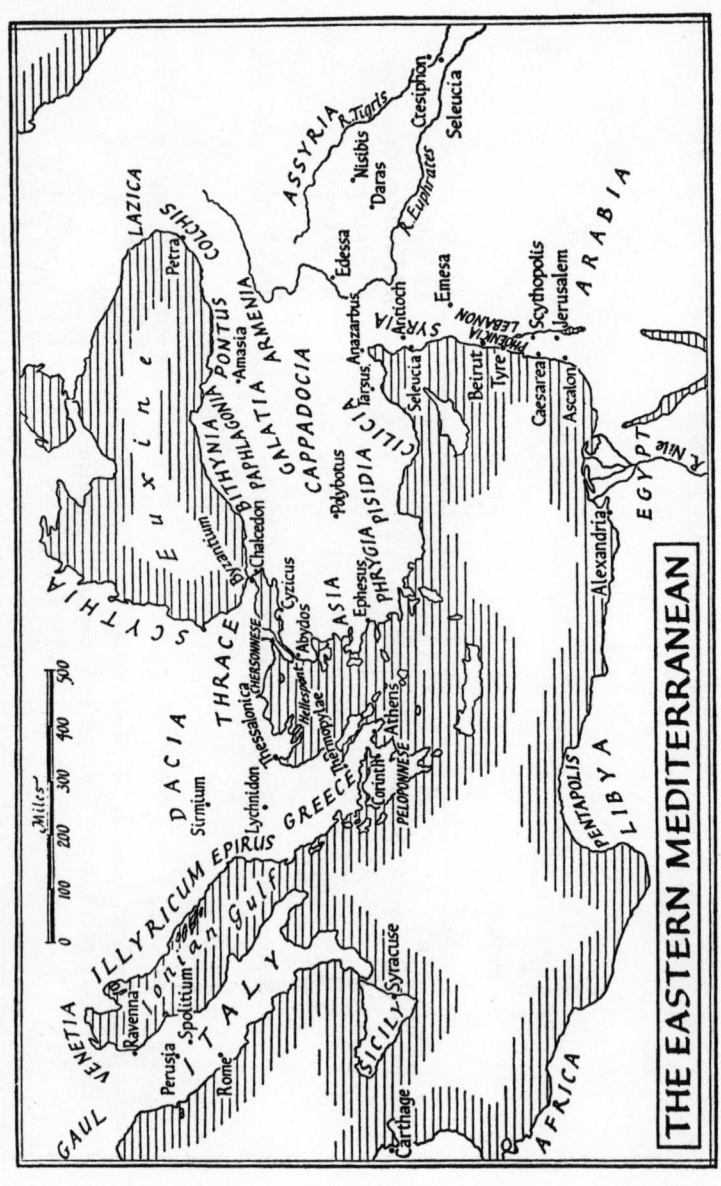

THE EASTERN MEDITERRANEAN

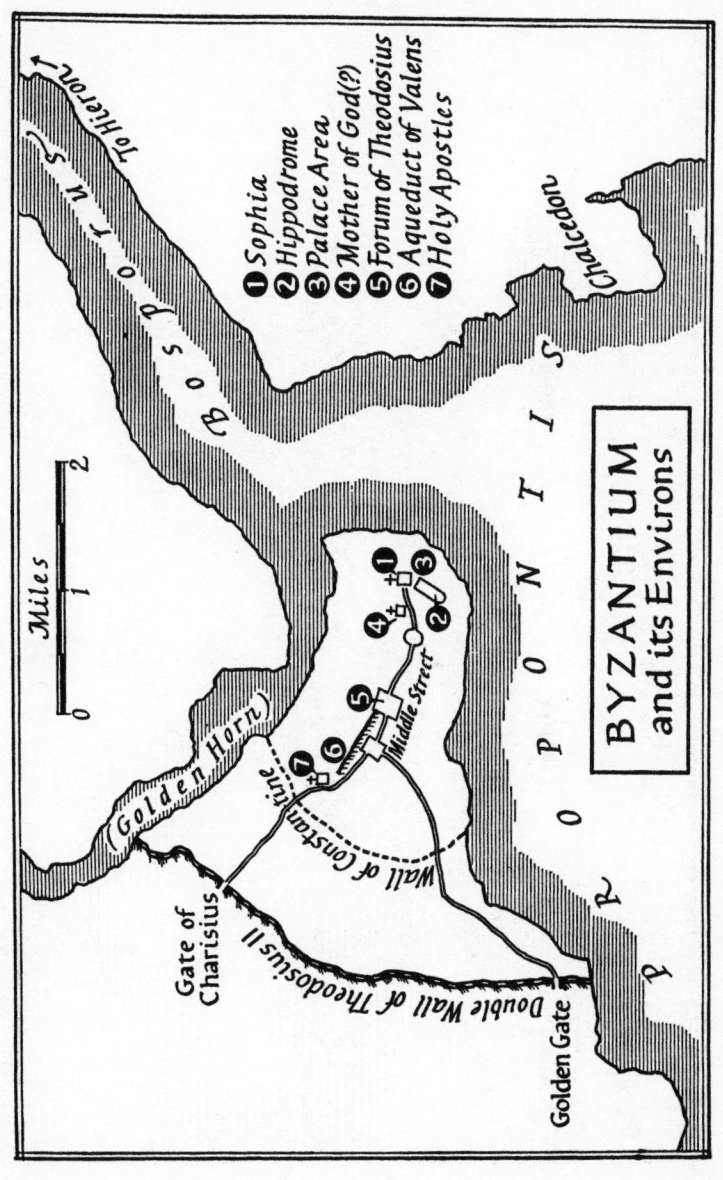

BYZANTIUM and its Environs

① Sophia
② Hippodrome
③ Palace Area
④ Mother of God (?)
⑤ Forum of Theodosius
⑥ Aqueduct of Valens
⑦ Holy Apostles

To Hieron
BOSPORUS
Chalcedon
PROPONTIS
(Golden Horn)
Miles
Gate of Charisius
Double Wall of Theodosius II
Golden Gate
Wall of Constantine
Middle Street

Index of Places

Index of Persons

Index of Subjects

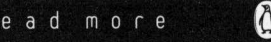

PENGUIN CLASSICS

THE RISE OF THE ROMAN EMPIRE   POLYBIUS

'If history is deprived of the truth, we are left with nothing but an idle, unprofitable tale.'

In writing his account of the relentless growth of the Roman Empire, the Greek statesman Polybius (*c.* 200–118 BC) set out to help his fellow-countrymen understand how their world came to be dominated by Rome. Opening with the Punic War in 264 BC, he vividly records the critical stages of Roman expansion: its campaigns throughout the Mediterranean, the temporary setbacks inflicted by Hannibal and the final destruction of Carthage in 146 BC. An active participant in contemporary politics, as well as a friend of many prominent Roman citizens, Polybius was able to draw on a range of eyewitness accounts and on his own experiences of many of the central events, giving his work immediacy and authority.

Ian Scott-Kilvert's translation fully preserves the clarity of Polybius's narrative. This substantial selection of the surviving volumes is accompanied by an introduction by F. W. Walbank, which examines Polybius's life and times, and the sources and technique he employed in writing his history.

Translated by Ian Scott-Kilvert
Selected with an introduction by F. W. Walbank

PENGUIN CLASSICS

THE POLITICS ARISTOTLE

'Man is by nature a political animal'

In *The Politics* Aristotle addresses the questions that lie at the heart of political science. How should society be ordered to ensure the happiness of the individual? Which forms of government are best and how should they be maintained? By analysing a range of city constitutions – oligarchies, democracies and tyrannies – he seeks to establish the strengths and weaknesses of each system to decide which are the most effective, in theory and in practice. A hugely significant work, which has influenced thinkers as diverse as Aquinas and Machiavelli, *The Politics* remains an outstanding commentary on fundamental political issues and concerns, and provides fascinating insights into the workings and attitudes of the Greek city-state.

The introductions by T. A. Sinclair and Trevor J. Saunders discuss the influence of *The Politics* on philosophers, its modern relevance and Aristotle's political beliefs. This edition contains Greek and English glossaries, and a bibliography for further reading.

Translated by T. A. Sinclair
Revised and re-presented by Trevor J. Saunders

PENGUIN CLASSICS

THE BIRDS AND OTHER PLAYS   ARISTOPHANES

THE KNIGHTS / PEACE / THE BIRDS / THE ASSEMBLYWOMEN / WEALTH

'Oh wings are splendid things, make no mistake: they really help you rise in the world'

The plays collected in this volume, written at different times in Aristophanes's forty-year career as a dramatist, all contain his trademark bawdy comedy and dazzling verbal agility. In *The Birds*, two frustrated Athenians join with the birds to build the utopian city of 'Much Cuckoo in the Clouds'. *The Knights* is a venomous satire on Cleon, the prominent Athenian demagogue, while *The Assemblywomen* considers the war of the sexes, as the women of Athens infiltrate the all-male Assembly in disguise. The lengthy conflict with Sparta is the subject of *Peace*, inspired by the hope of a settlement in 421 BC, and *Wealth* reflects the economic catastrophe that hit Athens after the war, as the god of riches is depicted as a ragged, blind old man.

The lively translations by David Barrett and Alan H. Sommerstein capture the full humour of the plays. The introduction examines Aristophanes's life and times, and the comedy and poetry of his works. This volume also includes an introductory note for each play.

Translated with an introduction by David Barrett and Alan H. Sommerstein

PENGUIN CLASSICS

THE ANNALS OF IMPERIAL ROME   TACITUS

'Nero was already corrupted by every lust, natural and unnatural'

The Annals of Imperial Rome recount the major historical events from the years shortly before the death of Augustus to the death of Nero in AD 68. With clarity and vivid intensity Tacitus describes the reign of terror under the corrupt Tiberius, the great fire of Rome during the time of Nero and the wars, poisonings, scandals, conspiracies and murders that were part of imperial life. Despite his claim that the *Annals* were written objectively, Tacitus's account is sharply critical of the emperors' excesses and fearful for the future of imperial Rome, while also filled with a longing for its past glories.

Michael Grant's fine translation captures the moral tone, astringent wit and stylish vigour of the original. His introduction discusses the life and works of Tacitus and the historical context of the *Annals*. This edition also contains a key to place names and technical terms, maps, tables and suggestions for further reading.

Translated with an introduction by Michael Grant

PENGUIN CLASSICS

THE AGRICOLA *AND* THE GERMANIA   TACITUS

'Happy indeed were you, Agricola, not only in your glorious life but in your timely death'

The Agricola is both a portrait of Julius Agricola – the most famous governor of Roman Britain and Tacitus's well-loved and respected father-in-law – and the first detailed account of Britain that has come down to us. It offers fascinating descriptions of the geography, climate and peoples of the country, and a succinct account of the early stages of the Roman occupation, nearly fatally undermined by Boudicca's revolt in AD 61 but consolidated by campaigns that took Agricola as far as Anglesey and northern Scotland. The warlike German tribes are the focus of Tacitus's attention in *The Germania*, which, like *The Agricola*, often compares the behaviour of 'barbarian' peoples favourably with the decadence and corruption of Imperial Rome.

Harold Mattingly's translation brings Tacitus's extravagant imagination and incisive wit vividly to life. In his introduction, he examines Tacitus's life and literary career, the governorship of Agricola and the political background of Rome's rapidly expanding empire. This edition also includes a select bibliography, and maps of Roman Britain and Germany.

Translated with an introduction by H. Mattingly
Translation revised by S. A. Handford

PENGUIN CLASSICS

METAMORPHOSES   OVID

'Her soft white bosom was ringed in a layer
of bark, her hair was turned into foliage, her arms into branches'

Ovid's sensuous and witty poem brings together a dazzling array of
mythological tales, ingeniously linked by the idea of transformation –
often as a result of love or lust – where men and women find themselves
magically changed into new and sometimes extraordinary beings.
Beginning with the creation of the world and ending with the deification
of Augustus, Ovid interweaves many of the best-known myths and
legends of ancient Greece and Rome, including the stories of Daedalus
and Icarus, Pyramus and Thisbe, Pygmalion, Perseus and Andromeda,
and the Fall of Troy. Erudite but light-hearted, dramatic and yet playful,
the *Metamorphoses* has influenced writers and artists throughout the
centuries from Shakespeare and Titian to Picasso and Ted Hughes.

This lively, accessible new translation by David Raeburn is in hexameter
verse form, which brilliantly captures the energy and spontaneity of the
original. The edition contains an introduction discussing the life and work
of Ovid as well as a preface to each book, explanatory notes and an index
of people, gods and places.

A new verse translation by David Raeburn with an introduction by
Denis Feeney

PENGUIN CLASSICS

THE LETTERS OF THE YOUNGER PLINY

'Of course these details are not important enough for history ... you have only yourself to blame for asking for them'

A prominent lawyer and administrator, Pliny (*c.* AD 61–113) was also a prolific letter-writer, who numbered among his correspondents such eminent figures as Tacitus, Suetonius and the Emperor Trajan, as well as a wide circle of friends and family. His lively and very personal letters address an astonishing range of topics, from a deeply moving account of his uncle's death in the eruption that engulfed Pompeii and observations on the early Christians – 'a desperate sort of cult carried to extravagant lengths' – to descriptions of everyday life in Rome, with its scandals and court cases, and of his own life in the country. Providing a series of fascinating views of imperial Rome, his letters also offer one of the fullest self-portraits to survive from classical times.

Betty Radice's definitive edition was the first complete modern translation of Pliny's letters. In her introduction, she examines the shrewd, tolerant and occasionally pompous man who emerges from these.

Translated with an introduction by Betty Radice

PENGUIN CLASSICS

NATURAL HISTORY: A SELECTION
PLINY THE ELDER

'The world is the work of Nature and, at the same time, the embodiment of Nature herself'

Pliny's *Natural History* is an astonishingly ambitious work that ranges from astronomy to art and from geography to zoology. Mingling acute observation with often wild speculation, it offers a fascinating view of the world as it was understood in the first century AD, whether describing the danger of diving for sponges, the first water-clock, or the use of asses' milk to remove wrinkles. Pliny himself died while investigating the volcanic eruption that destroyed Pompeii in AD 79, and the natural curiosity that brought about his death is also very much evident in the *Natural History* – a book that proved highly influential right up to the Renaissance and that his nephew, Pliny the younger, described 'as full of variety as nature itself'.

John F. Healy has made a fascinating and varied selection from the *Natural History* for this clear, modern translation. In his introduction, he discusses the book and its sources topic by topic. This edition also includes a full index and notes.

Translated with an introduction and notes by John F. Healy

read more 🐧

PENGUIN CLASSICS

THE ALEXIAD OF ANNA COMNENA

'The shining light of the world, the great Alexius'

Anna Comnena (1083–1153) wrote *The Alexiad* as an account of the reign of her father, the Byzantine Emperor Alexius I. It is also an important source of information on the Byzantine war with the Normans, and on the First Crusade in which Alexius participated. While the Byzantines were allied to the Crusaders, they were nonetheless critical of their behaviour and Anna's book offers a startlingly different perspective to that of Western historians. Her character sketches are shrewd and forthright – from the Norman invader Robert Guiscard ('nourished by manifold evil') and his son Bohemond ('like a streaking thunderbolt') to Pope Gregory VII ('unworthy of a high priest'). *The Alexiad* is a vivid and dramatic narrative, which reveals as much about the character of its intelligent and dynamic author as it does about the fascinating period through which she lived.

E. R. A. Sewter's translation captures all the strength and immediacy of the original and is complimented by an introduction, which examines Anna's life and times. This edition also includes maps, appendices, genealogical tables, a bibliography, and indexes of events and names.

Translated with an introduction by E. R. A. Sewter

PENGUIN CLASSICS

CITY OF GOD ST AUGUSTINE

'The Heavenly City outshines Rome, beyond comparison. There, instead of victory, is truth; instead of rank, holiness'

St Augustine, Bishop of Hippo, was one of the central figures in the history of Christianity, and *City of God* is one of his greatest theological works. Written as an eloquent defence of the faith at a time when the Roman Empire was on the brink of collapse, it examines the ancient pagan religions of Rome, the arguments of the Greek philosophers and the revelations of the Bible. Pointing the way forward to a citizenship that transcends the best political experiences of the world and offers citizenship that will last for eternity, *City of God* is one of the most influential documents in the development of Christianity.

This edition contains a new introduction that examines the text in the light of contemporary Greek and Roman thought and political change. It demonstrates the religious and literary influences on St Augustine and his significance as a Christian thinker. There is also a chronology and bibliography.

Translated with notes by Henry Bettenson with an introduction by Gill Evans

PENGUIN CLASSICS

BEOWULF

'With bare hands shall I
grapple with the fiend, fight to the death here,
hater and hated! He who is chosen
shall deliver himself to the Lord's judgement'

Beowulf is the greatest surviving work of literature in Old English,
unparalleled in its epic grandeur and scope. It tells the story of the heroic
Beowulf and of his battles, first with the monster Grendel, who has laid
waste to the great hall of the Danish king Hrothgar, then with Grendel's
avenging mother, and finally with a dragon that threatens to devastate his
homeland. Through its blend of myth and history, *Beowulf* vividly evokes
a twilight world in which men and supernatural forces live side by side,
and celebrates the endurance of the human spirit in a transient world.

Michael Alexander's landmark modern English verse translation has
been revised to take account of new readings and interpretations. His
new introduction discusses central themes of *Beowulf* and its place
among epic poems, the history of its publication and reception, and
issues of translation.

'A foundation stone of poetry in English' Andrew Motion

Translated with an introduction and notes by Michael Alexander

---

PENGUIN CLASSICS

THE DECAMERON GIOVANNI BOCCACCIO

'Ever since the world began, men have been subject to various tricks of Fortune'

In the summer of 1348, as the Black Death ravages their city, ten young Florentines take refuge in the countryside. They amuse themselves by each telling a story a day for the ten days they are destined to remain there – a hundred stories of love, adventure and surprising twists of fate. Less preoccupied with abstract concepts of morality or religion than earthly values, the tales range from the bawdy Peronella hiding her lover in a tub to Ser Cepperallo, who, despite his unholy effrontery, becomes a Saint. The result is a towering monument of European literature and a masterpiece of imaginative narrative.

This is the second edition of G. H. McWilliam's acclaimed translation of *The Decameron*. In his introduction Professor McWilliam illuminates the worlds of Boccaccio and of his storytellers, showing Boccaccio as a master of vivid and exciting prose fiction.

Translated with a new introduction and notes by G. H. McWilliam

THE STORY OF PENGUIN CLASSICS

Before 1946 ... 'Classics' are mainly the domain of academics and students; readable editions for everyone else are almost unheard of. This all changes when a little-known classicist, E. V. Rieu, presents Penguin founder Allen Lane with the translation of Homer's *Odyssey* that he has been working on in his spare time.

1946 Penguin Classics debuts with *The Odyssey*, which promptly sells three million copies. Suddenly, classics are no longer for the privileged few.

1950s Rieu, now series editor, turns to professional writers for the best modern, readable translations, including Dorothy L. Sayers's *Inferno* and Robert Graves's unexpurgated *Twelve Caesars*.

1960s The Classics are given the distinctive black covers that have remained a constant throughout the life of the series. Rieu retires in 1964, hailing the Penguin Classics list as 'the greatest educative force of the twentieth century.'

1970s A new generation of translators swells the Penguin Classics ranks, introducing readers of English to classics of world literature from more than twenty languages. The list grows to encompass more history, philosophy, science, religion and politics.

1980s The Penguin American Library launches with titles such as *Uncle Tom's Cabin*, and joins forces with Penguin Classics to provide the most comprehensive library of world literature available from any paperback publisher.

1990s The launch of Penguin Audiobooks brings the classics to a listening audience for the first time, and in 1999 the worldwide launch of the Penguin Classics website extends their reach to the global online community.

The 21st Century Penguin Classics are completely redesigned for the first time in nearly twenty years. This world-famous series now consists of more than 1300 titles, making the widest range of the best books ever written available to millions – and constantly redefining what makes a 'classic'.

The Odyssey continues ...

The best books ever written

PENGUIN 🐧 CLASSICS

SINCE 1946

Find out more at www.penguinclassics.com